This Book Belongs To:

* *

Christmas 2010

2010

Christmas

with Southern Living®

2010 Christmas
with Southern Living®

Oxmoor
House®

©2010 by Oxmoor House, Inc.
P.O. Box 360220, Des Moines, IA 50336-0220

ISBN-13: 978-0-8487-3346-9
ISBN-10: 0-8487-3346-0
ISSN: 0747-7791

Printed in the United States of America
First Printing 2010

Oxmoor House, Inc.
VP, Publishing Director: Jim Childs
Editorial Director: Susan Payne Dobbs
Brand Manager: Daniel Fagan
Managing Editor: Laurie S. Herr

Christmas with Southern Living 2010
Senior Editor: Rebecca Brennan
Project Editor: Diane Rose
Contributing Writer: Katherine Cobbs
Director, Test Kitchens: Elizabeth Tyler Austin
Assistant Director, Test Kitchens: Julie Christopher
Test Kitchens Professionals: Allison E. Cox, Julie Gunter,
    Kathleen Royal Phillips, Catherine Crowell Steele, Ashley T. Strickland
Photography Director: Jim Bathie
Senior Photo Stylist: Kay E. Clarke
Associate Photo Stylist: Katherine Eckert Coyne
Senior Production Manager: Greg A. Amason

Contributors
Designer: Carol Damsky
Copy Editor: Julie Gillis
Proofreader: Donna Baldone
Indexer: Mary Ann Laurens
Interns: Ina Ables, Sarah M. Belanger, Georgia Dodge, Maggie McDaris,
    Chris Cosgrove, Perri K. Hubbard
Photographer: Lee Harrelson

To order additional publications, call 1-800-765-6400 or 1-800-491-0551.

For more books to enrich your life, visit **oxmoorhouse.com**

To search, savor, and share thousands of recipes, visit **myrecipes.com**

Cover: Hot Mocha (page 26), Petits Cakes (page 162), Candy Bar Sugar
    Cookies (page 165)
Back Cover: wreath (page 80), Bananas Foster Cake (page 50), hanging basket
    (page 118)

Welcome

With this 30th anniversary edition of *Christmas with Southern Living*, we offer you our favorite yuletide inspirations. Whether you're looking for casual entertaining menus or a special dish for a relaxing weeknight meal, you'll find the perfect recipes for every occasion from our selection of over 100 all-new, kitchen-tested, and guaranteed-to-please recipes.

For the home, we show dozens of ways to decorate with seasonal style—many with natural materials you'll find in your backyard. As for your gift list? We've got you covered there, too. Bite-sized food gifts and do-it-yourself spa gifts offer a variety of treats for body and soul that are perfect for packaging.

Thanks for allowing us to share the holidays with you.

With warm wishes for a special season,

Rebecca Brennan

Rebecca Brennan
Senior Editor

CONTENTS

Easy
ENTERTAINING

Share the holiday spirit with friends and family. The six menus on the following pages provide you with all you need to make planning a breeze—including easy-to-use game plans.

make-ahead PROGRESSIVE DINNER

A progressive dinner lets hosts divide and conquer. Setting the scene and mastering a single dish is all that's required before the party moves to the next home on the menu.

menu

SWEET TEA AND LIMONCELLO MARTINIS

LAMB SLIDERS WITH MINT-GARLIC MAYONNAISE

HEARTS OF ROMAINE WITH MOLASSES VINAIGRETTE AND
PARMESAN-PANCETTA CRISPS

ROASTED MEYER LEMON-PEPPERCORN GAME HENS

STUFFED PORK LOIN CHOPS

CRISPY SAGE AND GARLIC SMASHED BABY
RED POTATOES

ROASTED ROOT VEGETABLES WITH PRALINE CRUNCH

GINGERSNAP AND POACHED PEAR TRIFLE

CHOCOLATE CHUNK CHEESECAKE

serves 12

game plan

up to 1 week ahead:

☐ Prepare Molasses Vinaigrette; cover and chill.

☐ Chop vegetables for Praline Roasted Root Vegetables and store in a large airtight container.

☐ Prepare Praline Crunch; store in an airtight container.

2 days ahead:

☐ Prepare, cover, and chill Mint-Garlic Mayonnaise.

☐ Prepare and brine game hens.

☐ Cook and mash potatoes; cover and chill.

☐ Prepare poached pears; cover and chill.

1 day ahead:

☐ Combine and chill ingredients for Sweet Tea and Limoncello Martinis.

☐ Prepare patties for Lamb Sliders; cover and chill.

☐ Prepare Parmesan-Pancetta Crisps; store in an airtight container.

☐ Prepare trifle; cover and chill.

☐ Prepare Chocolate Chunk Cheesecake; cover loosely with plastic wrap, and chill.

4 hours ahead:

☐ Remove hens from brine. Tie with strings and arrange on baking sheets; chill.

2 hours ahead:

☐ Prepare Roasted Meyer Lemon-Peppercorn Game Hens. Cover and keep warm.

☐ Stuff pork loin chops.

1 hour ahead:

☐ Prepare Lamb Sliders.

☐ Prepare Roasted Root Vegetables.

30 minutes ahead:

☐ Fry sage and garlic for Crispy Sage and Garlic Smashed Baby Red Potatoes.

10 minutes ahead:

☐ Arrange salads on serving plates.

☐ Reheat potatoes in microwave.

when guests arrive:

☐ Finish Sun-dried Tomato and Goat Cheese-Stuffed Pork Loin Chops.

*This game plan is set up as if the menu is being prepared at one location. For a progressive-style dinner, assign and prepare recipes accordingly.

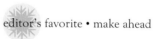

make ahead • quick & easy

Sweet Tea and Limoncello Martinis

MAKES 12 SERVINGS
HANDS-ON TIME: 4 MIN.; TOTAL TIME: 2 HR., 4 MIN.

6 cups cold sweetened tea
3 cups vodka
1½ cups limoncello
Garnish: lemon twists

1. Combine first 3 ingredients in a large pitcher. Cover and chill thoroughly. Serve in chilled martini glasses. Garnish, if desired.

2. For each serving, fill a martini shaker half full of crushed ice. Add ¾ cup tea mixture. Cover with lid, and shake until thoroughly chilled. Remove lid, and strain into a chilled martini glass. Garnish, if desired, and serve immediately.

editor's favorite • make ahead

Lamb Sliders

MAKES 2 DOZEN
HANDS-ON TIME: 23 MIN.; TOTAL TIME: 27 MIN.

Regular slider buns were too big for these tiny sandwiches, so we used dinner rolls instead.

1 large egg
1 lb. ground lamb
½ cup soft, fresh white-wheat breadcrumbs (1 slice)
3 Tbsp. chopped fresh flat-leaf parsley
½ tsp. kosher salt
½ tsp. freshly ground pepper
2 garlic cloves, minced
2 shallots, minced
1 English cucumber
24 (2½-inch) dinner rolls, halved and toasted
Mint-Garlic Mayonnaise

1. Preheat broiler with oven rack 3 inches from heat. Whisk egg in a medium bowl. Add lamb and next 6 ingredients; combine, using hands. Shape mixture into 24 (2-inch) patties. Place patties on a lightly greased jelly-roll pan. Broil 3 to 4 minutes or until done.

2. Meanwhile, cut 24 thin slices from cucumber, reserving remaining cucumber for another use.

3. Spread cut sides of rolls with Mint-Garlic Mayonnaise. Place patties on bottoms of rolls; top with cucumber slices and roll tops.

Sweet Tea and
Limoncello Martinis;
Lamb Sliders

Mint-Garlic Mayonnaise

MAKES ABOUT ½ CUP
HANDS-ON TIME: 5 MIN.; TOTAL TIME: 5 MIN.

- ½ cup mayonnaise
- 1½ Tbsp. minced fresh mint
- 1½ tsp. fresh lemon juice
- ½ tsp. lemon zest
- ¼ tsp. kosher salt
- ⅛ tsp. ground red pepper
- 2 garlic cloves, minced

1. Stir together all ingredients in a small bowl. Cover and chill until ready to use.

make ahead:

Cover and chill patties up to 24 hours ahead.
Prepare, cover, and chill Mint-Garlic Mayonnaise up
to 2 days ahead.

editor's favorite • make ahead

Hearts of Romaine With Molasses Vinaigrette and Parmesan-Pancetta Crisps

MAKES 12 SERVINGS
HANDS-ON TIME: 18 MINUTES; TOTAL TIME: 1 HR., 14 MIN.

6   romaine lettuce hearts
Ice water
Molasses Vinaigrette
Parmesan-Pancetta Crisps

1. Cut lettuce hearts in half lengthwise, leaving stem intact. Plunge into ice water to cover; let stand 30 minutes. Drain well, and pat dry with paper towels. Cover and chill until ready to serve.

2. Trim 3 inches from stem end of each lettuce heart half, and arrange on each of 12 serving plates. Drizzle with desired amount of Molasses Vinaigrette, and serve immediately with Parmesan-Pancetta Crisps.

make ahead:

The lettuce, vinaigrette, and crisps can be prepared a day ahead, if desired. Prepare the vinaigrette while the lettuce stands in the ice water. Assemble salad just before serving.

Molasses Vinaigrette

MAKES 2½ CUPS
HANDS-ON TIME: 5 MIN. TOTAL TIME: 5 MIN.

½   cup sherry vinegar
½   cup chopped fresh flat-leaf parsley
¼   cup light molasses
2   tsp. salt
1   tsp. freshly ground pepper
3   shallots, minced
1   cup extra virgin olive oil

1. Combine first 6 ingredients in a medium bowl; gradually whisk in olive oil. Cover and chill up to 1 week.

Parmesan-Pancetta Crisps

MAKES 2 DOZEN
HANDS-ON TIME: 14 MIN.; TOTAL TIME: 30 MIN. (8 MIN. PER BATCH)

2   oz. (⅛-inch-thick) slices pancetta, minced
    (about 6 Tbsp.)
4   oz. Parmesan cheese, grated
Parchment paper

1. Preheat oven to 400°. Cook pancetta in a large nonstick skillet over medium-high heat 7 minutes or until crisp, stirring occasionally; remove pancetta, and drain on paper towels.

2. Spoon cheese by about 1 Tbsp. into 28 portions 2 inches apart on large baking sheets lined with parchment paper; flatten each portion slightly, and sprinkle with pancetta. Bake at 400° for 5 to 8 minutes or until lightly browned and crisp. Immediately transfer crisps to a wire rack, using a spatula; let cool completely.

Roasted Meyer Lemon-Pepper-
corn Game Hen; Crispy Sage
and Garlic Smashed Baby
Red Potatoes; Roasted
Root Vegetables With
Praline Crunch

Roasted Meyer Lemon-Peppercorn Game Hens

MAKES 12 SERVINGS
HANDS-ON TIME: 1 HR., 5 MIN.; TOTAL TIME: 9 HR., 55 MIN.

These succulent little birds are worth the wait; the overnight brining makes them tender and juicy.

 1 cup kosher salt
 1 cup sugar
 2 Meyer lemons, thinly sliced
 2 tsp. freshly ground mixed peppercorns*
 4 bay leaves
 3 qt. ice water
12 (1½-lb.) Cornish hens
 2 Tbsp. Meyer lemon zest
 2 Tbsp. freshly ground mixed peppercorns
 ¼ cup butter, melted

1. Bring 1 qt. water, kosher salt, and next 4 ingredients to a boil in a large stockpot over medium-high heat. Reduce heat, and simmer 30 minutes. Stir in 3 qt. ice water. Rinse hens; pat dry, and add to brine. Cover and chill 8 hours or overnight.
2. Preheat oven to 425°. Remove hens from brine; pat dry. Tuck wing tips under. Tie legs together with string. Stir together lemon zest and 2 Tbsp. mixed peppercorns; rub spice mixture on all sides of hens. Arrange hens on racks in 2 large foil-lined rimmed baking sheets. Brush with melted butter.
3. Bake at 425° for 50 minutes or until hens are done. Cover and let stand 15 minutes before serving.

*We tested with Alessi Tip N' Grind Whole Mixed Peppercorns.

make ahead:

Brine hens up to 2 days ahead. Remove from brine; pat dry, and prepare for baking. Cover and chill until ready to bake.

Stuffed Pork Loin Chops

editor's favorite • make ahead

Stuffed Pork Loin Chops

MAKES 8 SERVINGS
HANDS-ON TIME: 31 MIN.; TOTAL TIME: 1 HR., 56 MIN

  1 Tbsp. oil from sun-dried tomatoes
  8 sun-dried tomatoes in oil, drained and minced
  2 garlic cloves, minced
  1 tsp. salt, divided
  1 tsp. freshly ground pepper, divided
  2 tsp. minced fresh thyme, divided
  ½ cup Japanese breadcrumbs (panko)
  ½ cup (4 oz.) crumbled goat cheese
  2 Tbsp. shredded Parmesan cheese
  8 (1-inch-thick) boneless pork loin chops
  2 Tbsp. olive oil, divided
  2 cups chicken broth
  2 tsp. lemon zest
  4 tsp. Dijon mustard
  2 Tbsp. fresh lemon juice
  2 Tbsp. butter

1. Heat sun-dried tomato oil in a large nonstick skillet; add tomatoes, garlic, ½ tsp. salt, ½ tsp. pepper, and 1 tsp. thyme. Sauté 2 minutes; transfer tomato mixture to a bowl. Stir in breadcrumbs and cheeses.

2. Cut a slit (about 2 inches deep and 3 inches long; do not cut in half) in thick side of each pork chop to form a pocket. Spoon 2 Tbsp. goat cheese mixture in each pocket. Pinch edges to seal. Sprinkle pork with remaining ½ tsp. salt and ½ tsp. pepper. Cover and chill 1 hour.

3. Preheat oven to 450°. Heat 1 Tbsp. olive oil in a large non-stick skillet over medium-high heat. Add half of pork; cook 2 minutes on each side. Place pork on a cooling rack in a rimmed baking sheet. Repeat procedure with remaining oil and pork. Bake at 450° for 25 minutes or until a thermometer inserted in center registers 155°.

4. Meanwhile, stir together remaining 1 tsp. thyme, 2 cups chicken broth, and next 3 ingredients in a small bowl; add to pan, stirring to loosen browned bits. Bring to a boil; reduce heat, and simmer 7 minutes or until slightly thickened. Stir in butter. Serve pork with sauce.

make ahead:

Prepare and chill pork chops as directed, setting drippings aside. When guests arrive, place pork in oven to bake. Reheat drippings while pork bakes; finish sauce.

editor's favorite • make ahead

Crispy Sage and Garlic Smashed Baby Red Potatoes

(pictured on page 15)

MAKES 12 SERVINGS
HANDS-ON TIME: 10 MIN.; TOTAL TIME: 54 MIN.

  6 lb. small red potatoes, halved (about 40 potatoes)
  2 cups milk
  ⅓ cup butter, melted
  2 tsp. kosher salt
 1½ tsp. freshly ground pepper
  4 garlic cloves, minced
  ½ cup extra virgin olive oil
 12 large garlic cloves, thinly sliced
 20 large fresh sage leaves

1. Cook potatoes in boiling salted water to cover in a large Dutch oven 20 minutes or until potato is tender. Drain; return potatoes to pan.

2. Combine milk and next 4 ingredients in a 4-cup glass measuring cup. Microwave at HIGH 2 to 3 minutes or until butter melts. Add milk mixture to potato; mash with a potato masher to desired consistency. Cover and keep warm.

3. Heat oil in a small skillet over medium-low heat; add garlic slices, and fry 2 to 3 minutes or until lightly browned. Remove garlic from oil, using a slotted spoon; drain on paper towels.

4. Increase heat to medium; add half of sage leaves. Fry 45 seconds or until crisp and browned. Remove sage leaves from oil, using a slotted spoon. Drain on paper towels. Repeat procedure with remaining half of sage leaves. Remove pan from heat; let oil cool 10 minutes.

5. Crumble sage leaves slightly. Before serving, drizzle oil over potatoes; sprinkle with sage leaves and garlic slices.

make ahead:

Cook and mash potato as directed up to 2 days ahead. Cover and chill. Just before serving, reheat potato in microwave, and fry garlic slices and sage leaves to complete recipe as directed.

Roasted Root Vegetables With Praline Crunch

(pictured on page 15)

MAKES 12 SERVINGS
HANDS-ON TIME: 5 MIN.; TOTAL TIME: 1 HR., 33 MIN.

- 2 lb. carrots, peeled, halved lengthwise, and cut into 2-inch pieces
- 2 lb. parsnips, peeled, halved lengthwise, and cut into 2-inch pieces
- 2 large red onions, halved lengthwise and cut into 1-inch wedges
- ½ cup extra virgin olive oil
- 1 Tbsp. kosher salt
- ½ tsp. freshly ground pepper
- Praline Crunch

1. Preheat oven to 425°. Combine first 6 ingredients in a large bowl, tossing to coat vegetables. Arrange in a single layer on 2 foil-lined rimmed baking sheets. Bake at 425° for 30 minutes. Stir and bake for 10 more minutes. Remove from oven. Sprinkle with Praline Crunch.

Praline Crunch

MAKES ABOUT 2 CUPS
HANDS-ON TIME: 5 MIN.; TOTAL TIME: 45 MIN.

- 1 cup sugar
- ¾ cup chopped pecans
- 1 tsp. kosher salt

1. Lightly grease a large baking sheet. Combine sugar and ¼ cup water in a medium skillet; cook over medium-high heat 8 minutes or until sugar caramelizes, tipping pan to incorporate mixture.
2. Stir in pecans and salt; remove from heat. Quickly spread mixture onto prepared pan. Cool completely. Peel Praline Crunch off baking sheet, break into large pieces, and chop. Store in an airtight container for up to 1 week.

make ahead

Gingersnap and Poached Pear Trifle

MAKES 10 SERVINGS
HANDS-ON TIME: 32 MIN.; TOTAL TIME: 8 HR., 32 MIN.

This dessert offers ample make-ahead opportunities, leaving simple assembly to be done shortly before guests arrive.

- 6 large ripe pears, peeled, cored, and cut into 1-inch cubes
- 2 cups Chardonnay or other dry white wine
- ½ cup sugar
- 1 (3-inch) cinnamon stick
- 1 vanilla bean, split lengthwise
- 1 whole clove
- 1 (4.6-oz) package vanilla-flavored cook-and-serve pudding mix
- 3 cups milk
- 1½ cups heavy cream
- 3 Tbsp. sugar
- 1 (1-lb.) package gingersnaps (we tested with Murray)

1. Bring pears and next 5 ingredients to a boil in a large saucepan over medium heat; reduce heat, and simmer 14 minutes or until pears are tender, stirring occasionally. Remove from heat. Transfer pears to a medium bowl, using a slotted spoon. Reserve pear syrup, discarding cinnamon stick and clove. Cover and chill syrup and pears 8 hours.
2. Prepare pudding mix according to package directions, using 3 cups milk. Place plastic wrap directly onto warm pudding (to prevent a film from forming), and chill thoroughly.
3. Scrape vanilla bean seeds into chilled pears, discarding vanilla bean.
4. Beat cream and 3 Tbsp. sugar in a medium bowl at high speed with an electric mixer until stiff peaks form.
5. Arrange one-fourth of gingersnaps in a 3-qt. trifle bowl, dipping each cookie quickly into pear syrup. Sprinkle with one-third of pears. Top with one-third of vanilla pudding and ½ cup sweetened whipped cream. Repeat layers twice, ending with gingersnaps and remaining sweetened whipped cream. Cover and chill 3 to 8 hours.

make ahead:

Chop vegetables and store in a large airtight container in the refrigerator up to 3 days ahead. Prepare and store Praline Crunch.

fix it faster:

Save time by using instant vanilla pudding mix or prepackaged vanilla pudding. You'll need 3 cups pudding.

Gingersnap and Poached
Pear Trifle

*Individual trifle bowls make serving dessert as easy as
it is to make.*

editor's favorite • make ahead

Chocolate Chunk Cheesecake

MAKES 12 SERVINGS
HANDS-ON TIME: 16 MIN.; TOTAL TIME: 1 HR., 26 MIN.

This highly rated dessert will satisfy chocolate and cheese-cake lovers alike with its creamy chocolate filling and bursts of chocolate chunks.

24	chocolate wafer cookies
2	Tbsp. sugar
¼	cup butter, melted
2½	(4-oz.) semisweet chocolate baking bars, divided*
3	(8-oz.) packages cream cheese, softened
½	cup sour cream, at room temperature
1	tsp. vanilla extract
1	cup sugar
3	Tbsp. all-purpose flour
5	large eggs
1	(11.5-oz.) package chocolate chunks, divided*
¾	cup whipping cream

1. Preheat oven to 350°. Process cookies and 2 Tbsp. sugar in a food processor until cookies are coarsely crushed. With processor running, pour butter through food chute; process until cookies are finely crushed. Press mixture firmly on bottom of a lightly greased 9-inch springform pan. Place springform pan in a shallow baking pan. Bake at 350° for 10 minutes; let cool. Reduce oven temperature to 325°.

2. Break 1 baking bar into squares, and place in a microwave-safe bowl. Microwave at HIGH 1 minute; stir until smooth. Beat cream cheese, sour cream, and vanilla at low speed with an electric mixer until creamy. Gradually beat in melted chocolate; beat in 1 cup sugar and flour. Add eggs, 1 at a time, beating just until yellow disappears. Stir in 1 cup chocolate chunks.

3. Pour batter into baked crust; sprinkle with remaining chocolate chunks. Bake at 325° for 1 hour or until set.

4. Remove cheesecake from oven; gently run a knife around outer edge of cheesecake to loosen from sides of pan; cool completely on a wire rack. Cover and chill 8 hours.

5. Remove sides and bottom of pan; place cheesecake on a serving plate.

6. Chop remaining 1½ baking bars, and place in a microwave-safe bowl. Add whipping cream, and microwave at HIGH 1 minute. Stir until blended and smooth; let stand 5 minutes.

7. Pour ganache over chilled cheesecake, allowing ganache to spill over edges of cheesecake; smooth ganache with an offset spatula. Chill at least 1 hour before serving.

*We tested with Ghirardelli baking bars and Nestlé Toll House chocolate chunks.

You can prepare this cheesecake a day ahead. Just cover it loosely with plastic wrap, and chill.

Christmas
TREE-CUTTING PARTY

Let the tree trimming begin! Make a tradition of this simple menu of soul-satisfying comforts to be enjoyed while you select the pick of the forest.

Chunky Cowboy Chili, page 24;
Cornmeal Cheddar Scones, page 25

game plan

1 day ahead:
- ☐ Prepare Chunky Cowboy Chili. Cover and chill in an airtight container.
- ☐ Bake cookies for Cinnamon-Pecan Cookie S'mores.
- ☐ Organize marshmallows, chocolate bars, and roasting sticks for S'mores.

2 hours ahead:
- ☐ Prepare Cornmeal Cheddar Scones; wrap tightly in plastic wrap.

1 hour ahead:
- ☐ Prepare Hot Mocha and pour into a thermos.
- ☐ Reheat chili and pour into a thermos.
- ☐ Pack in a picnic basket.

editor's favorite • make ahead

Chunky Cowboy Chili

(pictured on page 23)

MAKES ABOUT 14 CUPS
HANDS-ON TIME: 52 MIN.; TOTAL TIME: 2 HR., 22 MIN.

The flavor of this chili, like many soups and stews, is better the next day.

- 2 Tbsp. canola oil, divided
- 4 lb. boneless chuck roast, cut into ½-inch pieces
- 1 large onion, chopped
- 1 green bell pepper, chopped
- 2 garlic cloves, minced
- 1 Tbsp. Worcestershire sauce
- 2 Tbsp. tomato paste
- 2 tsp. chili powder
- ¼ tsp. ground cumin
- 2 (14.5-oz.) cans petite diced tomatoes with jalapeños, undrained
- 2 (8-oz.) cans tomato sauce
- 1 (16-oz.) can red beans
- 1 (15-oz.) can whole kernel corn, drained
- 1 (12-oz.) bottle dark beer (we tested with Michelob AmberBock)

1. Heat 1 Tbsp. oil in a large Dutch oven over medium-high heat; add half of beef. Cook 12 minutes or until dark brown, turning after 5 minutes. Remove beef from pan, and keep warm. Repeat procedure with remaining half of beef.
2. Add remaining 1 Tbsp. oil to pan. Add onion, bell pepper, and garlic to pan. Sauté 5 minutes or until tender. Return beef and accumulated juices to pan. Stir in 1 cup water, Worcestershire sauce, and remaining ingredients. Bring to a boil; cover, reduce heat, and simmer 1 hour and 30 minutes or until beef is tender and chili is thick.

Cornmeal Cheddar Scones

MAKES 15 SCONES
HANDS-ON TIME: 20 MIN.; TOTAL TIME: 40 MIN.

Cornmeal provides a little crunch to these tender, cheesy brunch favorites. They also pair well with soups, stews, chili, or fried chicken.

2   cups all-purpose flour
¾   cup stone-ground cornmeal
1   Tbsp. sugar
1   Tbsp. baking powder
½   tsp. baking soda
½   tsp. salt
⅛   tsp. ground red pepper
¾   cup unsalted butter, cut into chunks
1   cup (4 oz.) shredded extra-sharp Cheddar cheese
1   large egg
¾   cup buttermilk
Parchment paper
Unsalted butter, melted
Sea salt

1. Preheat oven to 425°. Place first 7 ingredients in a food processor. Add ¾ cup butter; pulse 3 or 4 times or until mixture resembles coarse meal. Place flour mixture in a large bowl; stir in cheese. Whisk together egg and buttermilk until blended. Make a well in center of dry ingredients; add egg mixture, stirring just until dry ingredients are moistened.

2. Turn dough out onto a floured surface; knead lightly 3 or 4 times. Pat dough into a 10- x 7-inch rectangle. Cut into 15 squares. Place squares on a parchment-lined baking sheet. Brush tops with melted unsalted butter, and sprinkle with sea salt. Bake at 425° for 20 minutes or until golden.

editor's favorite

Cinnamon-Pecan Cookie S'mores

MAKES 8 SERVINGS
HANDS-ON TIME: 14 MIN.; TOTAL TIME: 33 MIN.

*This variation on the campfire staple is over the top,
thanks to the nutty homemade cookies that replace the
graham crackers.*

½ cup butter, softened
½ cup firmly packed dark brown sugar
¼ cup granulated sugar
1 large egg
1½ tsp. vanilla extract
1¼ cups all-purpose flour
1 tsp. baking powder
1 tsp. ground cinnamon
¼ tsp. salt
1 cup coarsely chopped pecans, toasted
1 (4-oz.) bittersweet chocolate baking bar (we tested
   with Ghirardelli)
8 large marshmallows

1. Preheat oven to 350°. Beat butter at medium speed with
an electric mixer until creamy; gradually add sugars, beating
well. Add egg and vanilla, beating well.
2. Combine flour and next 3 ingredients; add to butter
mixture. Beat at low speed until blended. Stir in pecans.
3. Divide dough into 16 equal portions; roll each portion
into a ball. Place balls 1 inch apart on lightly greased baking
sheets; flatten slightly.
4. Bake at 350° for 16 minutes or until lightly browned. Cool
cookies on pans 1 minute. Transfer cookies to wire racks.
Cool completely.
5. Preheat broiler. Separate chocolate bar into 8 squares.
Place a chocolate square on flat side of each of 8 cookies.
6. Place marshmallows on a baking sheet. Broil 3 minutes
or until puffed and toasted. Immediately transfer marshmallows to tops of chocolate squares, using a small spatula. Top
marshmallows with remaining cookies, flat sides down; press
down gently.

editor's favorite

Hot Mocha

MAKES ABOUT 10 CUPS
HANDS-ON TIME: 12 MIN.; TOTAL TIME: 12 MIN.

*Whether the Hot Mudslide version or the nonalcoholic one,
this comforting drink will warm you down to your toes.*

1 cup unsweetened cocoa
1 cup sugar
¼ cup instant espresso*
2 cups half-and-half
6 cups milk
4 tsp. vanilla extract
Sweetened whipped cream
Chocolate syrup

1. Whisk together first 4 ingredients in a large saucepan. Cook,
whisking constantly, over medium heat until sugar dissolves.
Whisk in milk; cook over medium-high heat, whisking constantly
5 minutes or until very hot. (Do not boil.) Whisk in vanilla.
2. Pour chocolate mixture into mugs; top with whipped cream,
and drizzle with chocolate syrup.

*Omit or substitute decaffeinated espresso for the youngsters.

Note: To make a Hot Mudslide, omit espresso. Stir ½ cup
Kahlúa, ½ cup Baileys Irish Crème, and, if desired, ¼ cup
vodka into the hot milk mixture along with the vanilla. Proceed
as directed.

Keep cocoa hot in a thermos while you search for a tree. Add whipped cream and syrup before serving.

Hot Mocha

Cinnamon-Pecan Cookie
S'mores

holiday
TEX-MEX PARTY

It's the perfect time of year for throwing a fiesta. Zesty chiles, tangy citrus, and hints of cinnamon come together in this casual menu. Olé!

menu

CRANBERRY-LIME MARGARITAS

SMOKY GUACAMOLE

SPICY QUESO DIP

CHICKEN MEATBALLS IN MOLE SAUCE

MEXICAN LASAGNA

BLACK BEANS WITH SAFFRON RICE

MINI CHURROS

MEXICAN CHOCOLATE BAR COOKIES WITH
BITTERSWEET CHOCOLATE FROSTING

PINEAPPLE AGUA FRESCA

serves 8

game plan

1 week ahead:

- [ ] Prepare sugar syrup for Cranberry-Lime Margaritas. Cover and chill.

2 days ahead:

- [ ] Prepare meatballs; cool and place in a large zip-top plastic freezer bag. Seal and freeze.
- [ ] Prepare Pineapple Agua Fresca; chill.

1 day ahead:

- [ ] Combine ingredients for margaritas.
- [ ] Prepare Mole Sauce; cover and chill.
- [ ] Assemble Mexican Lasagna; cover with plastic wrap, and chill.
- [ ] Thaw meatballs overnight in refrigerator.

4 hours ahead:

- [ ] Set up chips for Queso and Guacamole bar.
- [ ] Cook meatballs; keep warm in a slow cooker.

2 hours ahead:

- [ ] Prepare Black Beans With Saffron Rice; keep warm.
- [ ] Prepare Smoky Guacamole. Cover tightly with plastic wrap, and chill.
- [ ] Let lasagna come to room temperature; bake lasagna.

1 hour ahead:

- [ ] Prepare Spicy Queso Dip; keep warm in slow cooker.
- [ ] Prepare Mini Churros.

editor's favorite • quick & easy

Cranberry-Lime Margaritas

MAKES 13 CUPS
HANDS-ON TIME: 10 MIN.; TOTAL TIME: 30 MIN.

If you like frozen margaritas, try processing the margarita mixture with crushed ice in a blender.

- 1 cup sugar
- 1 cup fresh lime juice
- 1½ cups tequila
- ½ cup orange liqueur
- 1 (64-oz.) bottle cranberry juice cocktail (we tested with Ocean Spray)
- Lime wedges
- Coarse salt
- Garnish: additional lime wedges

1. Stir together sugar and 1 cup water in a small saucepan. Cook over medium heat until sugar dissolves. Remove from heat. Pour into a large pitcher; cover and chill 20 minutes.
2. Add lime juice and next 3 ingredients to sugar syrup in pitcher. Chill until ready to serve. Rub glass rims with lime wedges, and dip rims in salt. Serve margaritas over crushed ice. Garnish, if desired.

Smoky Guacamole

MAKES 2 CUPS
HANDS-ON TIME: 8 MIN.; TOTAL TIME: 8 MIN.

3 ripe avocados
1 Tbsp. chopped fresh cilantro
3 Tbsp. fresh lime juice
1 Tbsp. chipotle chile hot sauce (we tested with Tabasco)
½ tsp. salt
2 garlic cloves, minced
Garnish: 1 small canned chipotle chile pepper in adobo sauce, drained and sliced

1. Cut avocados in half. Scoop avocado pulp into bowl; mash with a fork or potato masher until almost smooth. Stir in cilantro and next 4 ingredients. Garnish, if desired.

Spicy Queso Dip

MAKES 4 CUPS
HANDS-ON TIME: 12 MIN.; TOTAL TIME: 18 MIN.

The diced jalapeños in this spicy dip really pack some heat. If you prefer milder fare, you may reduce or omit the peppers.

1 cup milk
8 oz. queso melt cheese, shredded
8 oz. white American cheese slices, diced
2 Tbsp. butter
1 cup finely chopped onion
1 garlic clove, minced
1 cup finely chopped seeded tomato
1 (4-oz.) can diced jalapeño peppers, drained
Tortilla chips

1. Combine first 3 ingredients in a 2-quart glass bowl. Microwave at HIGH 5 minutes or until creamy, stirring every minute.
2. Melt butter in a large skillet over medium-high heat. Add onion and garlic; sauté 3 minutes or until tender. Stir in tomato, and sauté 2 minutes or until onion is tender. Stir in jalapeño peppers.
3. Stir vegetable mixture into cheese mixture until blended. Transfer dip to a 2-qt. slow cooker. Heat on low or warm setting for up to 2 hours, stirring occasionally. Serve with tortilla chips.

Spoon prepared guacamole into empty avocado shells if you want to offer individual portions.

editor's favorite • make ahead

Chicken Meatballs in Mole Sauce

MAKES 16 APPETIZER SERVINGS
HANDS-ON TIME: 39 MIN.; TOTAL TIME: 1 HR., 59 MIN.

    1 large egg
    2 lb. ground chicken
    1 cup fine, dry breadcrumbs
    ¼ cup chopped fresh cilantro
    1 tsp. salt
    2 large garlic cloves, minced
       Mole Sauce

1. Whisk egg in a large bowl. Stir in chicken and next 4 ingredients. Cover and chill 20 minutes.
2. Preheat oven to 375°. Coat 2 racks and 2 large rimmed baking sheets with cooking spray; place racks in prepared pans. Shape chicken mixture into 1-inch balls; place on racks. Bake at 375° for 20 minutes.
3. Place meatballs in large Dutch oven; stir in Mole Sauce. Cook over medium heat until thoroughly heated. Transfer to a chafing dish or slow cooker, if desired. Serve hot.

editor's favorite • make ahead

Mole Sauce

MAKES 5 CUPS
HANDS-ON TIME: 23 MIN.; TOTAL TIME: 1 HR., 3 MIN.

    4 ancho chiles
  1½ cups chopped onion
    2 garlic cloves, minced
    2 Tbsp. vegetable oil
    ⅓ cup raisins
    ¼ cup slivered almonds, toasted
    1 Tbsp. toasted sesame seeds (we tested with
       McCormick)
    1 tsp. salt
    ½ tsp. ground cinnamon
    ¼ tsp. dried oregano
    ¼ tsp. ground cumin
    ⅛ tsp. ground cloves
    ⅛ tsp. ground coriander
    ⅛ tsp. anise seeds
    1 (14.5-oz.) can petite-cut diced tomatoes with
       jalapeños, undrained
    ½ cup chicken broth
    1 (1-oz.) square bittersweet chocolate, chopped

1. Remove stems and seeds from chiles; soak in hot water to cover in a medium bowl 30 minutes or until softened.
2. Meanwhile, sauté onion and garlic 3 minutes in oil in a large Dutch oven over medium heat until crisp-tender. Stir in raisins and next 9 ingredients; cook 2 minutes, stirring often.
3. Drain chiles, reserving ⅓ cup soaking liquid. Process chiles and reserved soaking liquid in a food processor until pureed. Press chile puree through a wire-mesh strainer into a large skillet to measure about ⅓ cup, using back of a spoon to remove skins. (Mixture will be very thick.) Discard skins and any seeds.
4. Process onion mixture, tomatoes, and chicken broth in a food processor until smooth; stir into chile puree. Add chocolate. Cook over medium heat, whisking constantly, 5 minutes or until chocolate melts.

make ahead:

Prepare meatballs up to 2 days ahead; cool and place in a large zip-top plastic freezer bag. Seal bag; freeze. Prepare Mole Sauce up to 1 day ahead; cover and chill. Thaw meatballs overnight in refrigerator. Combine meatballs and sauce in a 3-quart slow cooker; cover and cook on HIGH 2 hours or until thoroughly heated.

Mexican Lasagna

MAKES 8 SERVINGS
HANDS-ON TIME: 18 MIN.; TOTAL TIME: 1 HR., 6 MIN.

This twist on traditional lasagna is on the spicy side. Use mild pork sausage if you prefer a tamer casserole.

    ½ lb. hot ground pork sausage
    ½ lb. ground round
    1 (15-oz.) can ranch-style pinto beans, drained
    1 (10-oz.) can diced tomatoes and green chiles, drained
    1 tsp. garlic powder
    1 tsp. ground cumin
    ½ tsp. salt
    ½ tsp. pepper
    1 (10¾-oz.) can cream of celery soup
    1 (10¾-oz.) can cream of mushroom soup
    1 (10-oz.) can enchilada sauce
    9 (6-inch) corn tortillas, divided
    2 cups (8 oz.) shredded sharp Cheddar cheese
    2 cups (8 oz.) shredded Monterey Jack or pepper Jack
       cheese
    1 medium tomato, chopped
    4 green onions, chopped
    1 medium avocado, chopped

Mexican Lasagna

1. Preheat oven to 350°. Cook sausage and ground round in a large nonstick skillet over medium-high heat, stirring often until meat crumbles and is no longer pink; drain. Return meat to pan; stir in beans and next 5 ingredients. Cook 2 minutes or until thoroughly heated.

2. Stir together soups and enchilada sauce in a medium saucepan; cook, stirring constantly, 3 minutes or until thoroughly heated.

3. Spoon one-third of sauce into a lightly greased 13- x 9-inch baking dish; top with 3 tortillas. Spoon half of beef mixture and one-third of sauce over tortillas; sprinkle with half of Cheddar cheese. Top with 3 tortillas; repeat layers with remaining beef, sauce, Cheddar cheese, and tortillas, ending with tortillas. Sprinkle with 1 cup Monterey Jack cheese.

4. Cover loosely with foil. Bake at 350° for 20 minutes. Add remaining 1 cup Monterey Jack; bake, uncovered, 10 more minutes. Let stand 10 minutes. Top with tomato, green onion, and avocado.

editor's favorite

Black Beans With Saffron Rice

MAKES 10 TO 12 SERVINGS
HANDS-ON TIME: 25 MIN.; TOTAL TIME: 1 HR., 1 MIN.

We started with canned beans and a packaged rice mix for convenience and then added characteristic Mexican flavors to create this colorful traditional side.

1   (16-oz.) package saffron rice (we tested with Mahatma)
4   (15-oz.) cans black beans, divided
1   Tbsp. olive oil
1   medium onion, chopped
1   green bell pepper, chopped
1   jalapeño pepper, minced
3   garlic cloves, minced
1   (14.5-oz.) can diced tomatoes with green chiles
    (we tested with Del Monte)
1   (14-oz.) can chicken broth
1   Tbsp. tomato paste
1   Tbsp. fresh lime juice
2   Tbsp. chopped fresh cilantro
¼   tsp. salt
¼   tsp. pepper
Garnishes: additional chopped fresh cilantro, sour cream

1. Cook rice according to package directions; keep hot.
2. Rinse and drain 2 cans beans (do not drain remaining 2 cans).
3. Heat oil in a Dutch oven over medium-high heat. Add onion and next 3 ingredients; sauté 5 minutes or until tender. Stir in beans, tomatoes, and next 6 ingredients. Bring to a boil; reduce heat, and simmer, uncovered, 30 minutes, stirring occasionally. Serve over hot rice. Garnish, if desired.

Mini Churros

MAKES 30 CHURROS
HANDS-ON TIME: 30 MIN.; TOTAL TIME: 30 MIN.

Serve these crunchy strands with Hot Mocha (page 26),
or dip them in chocolate fondue.

Vegetable oil
½ cup sugar
1¼ tsp. ground cinnamon, divided
1 cup self-rising flour
3 Tbsp. sugar
3 Tbsp. butter
1 tsp. vanilla extract
2 large eggs

1. Pour oil into a Dutch oven to a depth of 3 inches. Heat oil to 360°.

2. Meanwhile, whisk together ½ cup sugar and 1 tsp. cinnamon in a shallow bowl; set aside. Combine flour and remaining ¼ tsp. cinnamon in a bowl.

3. Place 1 cup water, 3 Tbsp. sugar, and butter in a medium saucepan. Bring to a boil; remove from heat, and add flour mixture, all at once, stirring vigorously until mixture leaves sides of pan and forms a ball. Let stand 1 minute. Add vanilla. Add eggs, 1 at a time, beating vigorously with a wooden spoon until smooth after each addition.

3. Spoon batter into a pastry bag fitted with a ⅜-inch star tip. Pipe batter, 5 (3- or 4-inch-long) strips at a time, into hot oil. (Use a paring knife to release strips of batter from pastry tip into hot oil.) Fry 1 to 2 minutes on each side or until browned; drain on paper towels. Roll hot churros in reserved cinnamon-sugar mixture. Serve warm or at room temperature.

Mexican Chocolate Bar Cookies With
Bittersweet Chocolate Frosting

Mexican Chocolate Bar Cookies With Bittersweet Chocolate Frosting

MAKES 12 SERVINGS
HANDS-ON TIME: 19 MIN.; TOTAL TIME: 53 MIN.

- 1 cup butter, divided
- 60 vanilla wafers, crushed (about 2½ cups)
- 1 Tbsp. vanilla extract, divided
- 2 (2-oz.) dark chocolate bars with chiles and nibs, chopped*
- 2 large eggs
- ¾ cup firmly packed light brown sugar
- ½ cup granulated sugar
- 1½ cups all-purpose flour
- ⅓ cup unsweetened cocoa
- ½ tsp. salt
- 1½ tsp. baking powder
- 1½ tsp. ground cinnamon
- ¾ tsp. ancho chile pepper (we tested with McCormick)*
- 1 cup powdered sugar
- ½ cup bittersweet chocolate morsels, melted
- 3 Tbsp. milk

1. Preheat oven to 350°. Grease a 13- x 9-inch pan; dust with flour, shaking out excess.

2. Place ¼ cup butter, cut into 4 pieces, in a medium microwave-safe bowl. Cover and microwave at HIGH 40 seconds or until melted. Stir in cookie crumbs and 1½ tsp. vanilla. Press crumb mixture firmly into prepared pan. Bake at 350° for 10 minutes or until browned around edges; set aside.

3. Combine remaining ¾ cup butter, cut into 12 pieces, and chopped chocolate in a small microwave-safe bowl. Cover and microwave at HIGH 1 minute until melted; stir until smooth.

4. Beat eggs, sugars, and remaining 1½ tsp. vanilla at medium speed with an electric mixer until blended. Whisk together flour and next 5 ingredients in a bowl; gradually add to egg mixture, beating at low speed. Stir in chocolate mixture. (Batter will be thick.) Spoon batter over prepared crust, spreading to edges of pan.

5. Bake at 350° for 22 minutes. Cool in pan on a wire rack.

6. Whisk together powdered sugar, melted chocolate morsels, and milk in a medium bowl until smooth. Spread frosting over cooled cookie. Let stand until frosting is set. Cut into 12 bars.

*We tested with Dagoba Xocolatl chocolate bars, which can be found at Whole Foods Market and at www.dagobachocolate. com. You may substitute 1½ tsp. freshly ground black pepper for the ancho chile pepper, if desired.

editor's favorite • quick & easy

Pineapple Agua Fresca

MAKES ABOUT 6½ CUPS
HANDS-ON TIME: 24 MIN.; TOTAL TIME: 24 MIN.

Agua Fresca means fresh water. In Mexico on a hot summer day, you can purchase fresh fruit–flavored waters on nearly every street corner. We've chosen fresh pineapple, readily available at Christmastime, to flavor this thirst quencher for our spicy menu.

- 8½ cups cubed fresh pineapple (about 2 small)
- 1¼ cups sugar
- ¼ cup fresh lime juice
- 3 cups cold water
- Ice cubes (optional)
- Garnishes: lime wedges on long skewers, fresh mint sprigs

1. Combine first 4 ingredients in a large bowl. Process pineapple mixture in a blender in 3 batches until smooth.

2. Pour pineapple mixture through a wire-mesh strainer into a pitcher, using back of a spoon to squeeze out liquid to measure 6½ cups. Cover and chill thoroughly. Serve over ice cubes, and garnish, if desired.

Crescent City CLASSICS

Enjoy an elegant menu that pays homage to New Orleans with its piquant Cajun and refined French accents. Let the good times roll!

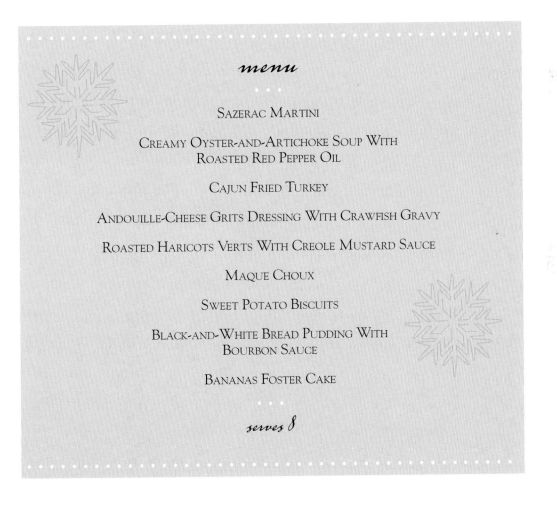

menu

SAZERAC MARTINI

CREAMY OYSTER-AND-ARTICHOKE SOUP WITH
ROASTED RED PEPPER OIL

CAJUN FRIED TURKEY

ANDOUILLE-CHEESE GRITS DRESSING WITH CRAWFISH GRAVY

ROASTED HARICOTS VERTS WITH CREOLE MUSTARD SAUCE

MAQUE CHOUX

SWEET POTATO BISCUITS

BLACK-AND-WHITE BREAD PUDDING WITH
BOURBON SAUCE

BANANAS FOSTER CAKE

serves 8

game plan

2 weeks ahead:
- Make grocery list. Shop for nonperishables.
- Plan table centerpiece and/or decorations.

1 week ahead:
- Prepare sugar syrup for martinis.
- Prepare Roasted Red Pepper Oil; chill.
- Prepare spice rub mixture for Cajun Fried Turkey; store in an airtight container.

3 or 4 days ahead:
- Finish remaining shopping.
- Place turkey in refrigerator to thaw, if frozen.
- Cube bread for bread pudding. Seal bread in a zip-top plastic bag.

2 days ahead:
- Prepare and chill grits for Andouille-Cheese Grits Dressing.
- Make cake layers, wrap in plastic wrap, and refrigerate.

1 day ahead:
- Inject turkey; cover and chill overnight.
- Prepare dressing, and spoon into a baking dish; cover and chill, unbaked, overnight.
- Prepare Creamy Oyster and Artichoke Soup up to before adding oysters; cover and chill.
- Make Brown Sugar Rum Glaze and frosting for cake. Assemble cake, cover loosely with plastic wrap, and chill.
- Make White Chocolate Bourbon Sauce for bread pudding; cover and chill.

4 hours ahead:
- Heat oil in turkey fryer.
- Rub turkey with spice rub mixture; place on fryer rod to drain.
- Let dressing come to room temperature.

- Prepare and bake bread pudding.

2 hours ahead:
- Fry turkey; let stand covered with aluminum foil.
- Bake Andouille-Cheese Grits Dressing; keep warm.
- Prepare Maque Choux; keep warm.
- Prepare Sweet Potato Biscuits

45 minutes ahead:
- Prepare Crawfish Gravy.
- Reheat soup.
- Prepare Roasted Haricots Verts With Creole Mustard Sauce.
- Take cake out of refrigerator and garnish.
- Reheat Black-and-White Bread Pudding and White Chocolate Bourbon Sauce.

10 minutes ahead:
- Add oysters to soup.

Sazerac Martini

MAKES 8 SERVINGS
HANDS-ON TIME: 7 MIN.

½ cup sugar
¼ cup absinthe
   Ice cubes
1½ cups rye whisky
8 dashes of bitters

1. Stir together sugar and ¼ cup water in a small saucepan. Cook over medium heat, stirring often, until sugar dissolves. Remove from heat; cool. Cover and chill.
2. Coat each of 8 chilled martini glasses with 1½ tsp. absinthe. Fill a martini shaker half full of ice. Add sugar mixture, whisky, and bitters. Cover with lid, and shake until thoroughly chilled. Remove lid, and strain into prepared glasses. Serve drink immediately.

Creamy Oyster-and-Artichoke Soup With Roasted Red Pepper Oil

MAKES 16 CUPS
HANDS-ON TIME: 10 MIN.; TOTAL TIME: 5 HR., 3 MIN.

2 (14-oz.) cans quartered artichoke hearts, drained
2½ tsp. salt, divided
1½ tsp. freshly ground pepper, divided
¼ cup butter
1 medium onion, finely chopped
3 celery ribs, finely chopped
4 garlic cloves, minced
1 cup all-purpose flour
2 (8-oz.) bottles clam juice
6 cups heavy cream
¼ tsp. ground red pepper
1 (1-qt.) container fresh standard oysters
3 Tbsp. butter
   Roasted Red Pepper Oil*

1. Preheat oven to 375°. Place artichokes in a single layer on a lightly greased large baking sheet. Sprinkle with 1 tsp. salt and ½ tsp. pepper. Bake at 375° for 18 minutes or until lightly browned.

2. Melt ¼ cup butter in a large Dutch oven over medium heat. Add onion, celery, and garlic; sauté 4 minutes. Stir in flour. Cook, stirring constantly, 1 minute. Gradually stir in clam juice, cream, remaining 1½ tsp. salt, remaining 1 tsp. pepper, artichokes, and ground red pepper; cook over medium heat, stirring often, 28 minutes or until thickened.
3. Add oysters and their liquid; cook 10 more minutes. Stir in 3 Tbsp. butter. Ladle soup into bowls; drizzle each serving with about ½ tsp. Roasted Red Pepper Oil.

*You may substitute oil from sun-dried tomatoes packed in oil or from red peppers packed in oil for the Roasted Red Pepper Oil, if desired.

Roasted Red Pepper Oil

MAKES 1 CUP
HANDS-ON TIME: 3 MIN.; TOTAL TIME: 4 HR., 3 MIN.

½ cup diced drained roasted red bell peppers
1 cup extra virgin olive oil

1. Place both ingredients in a small saucepan. Cook over medium-high heat 2 minutes or until thoroughly heated. Remove from heat; cover and let stand 4 hours.
2. Pour oil mixture through a wire-mesh strainer into sterilized decorative bottles, discarding solids. Seal bottles, and store in refrigerator.

Cajun Fried Turkey

MAKES 8 SERVINGS
HANDS-ON TIME: 41 MIN.; TOTAL TIME: 9 HR., 1 MIN.

It's easier to insert the thermometer into the thigh if the turkey is lowered into the hot oil upside down.

1 (12½-lb.) turkey
¼ cup chicken broth
¼ cup butter, melted
2 Tbsp. fresh lemon juice
1 Tbsp. hot sauce
2 tsp. garlic salt
3 Tbsp. paprika
2 tsp. salt
2 tsp. garlic powder
2 tsp. onion powder
1 tsp. ground red pepper
1 tsp. dried thyme leaves
1 tsp. dried oregano
1 tsp. coarsely ground pepper
3 to 4 gal. peanut oil

1. Remove giblets and neck from turkey; rinse with cold water. Drain well; pat dry.
2. Combine chicken broth and next 4 ingredients. Inject mixture into turkey using a meat injector. Cover and chill 8 hours.
3. Combine paprika and next 7 ingredients in a small bowl; rub in cavities and over surface of turkey. Place turkey, legs up, on fryer rod; allow liquid to drain for 20 to 30 minutes.
4. Meanwhile, pour oil into a deep propane turkey fryer 10 to 12 inches from top; heat oil to 375° over a medium-low flame according to manufacturer's instructions.
5. Carefully lower turkey into hot oil with rod attachment. Fry turkey 2 to 2½ minutes per pound or until a thermometer inserted in thigh registers 170°. (Keep oil temperature at 350°.)
6. Remove turkey from oil; drain well, and let cool slightly before slicing.

Andouille-Cheese Grits Dressing With Crawfish Gravy

MAKES 8 SERVINGS
HANDS-ON TIME: 50 MIN.; TOTAL TIME: 1 HR., 25 MIN.

To jump-start this recipe, prepare and chill the grits up to 2 days ahead.

3½ cups chicken broth
1½ cups uncooked quick-cooking grits
¼ tsp. ground red pepper
1 cup shredded sharp Cheddar cheese
1 Tbsp. olive oil
12 oz. andouille sausage, cut into bite-size pieces (2½ cups)
2 celery ribs, chopped
2 garlic cloves, minced
1 onion, chopped
1 small red bell pepper, chopped
¼ cup chopped fresh flat-leaf parsley
2 tsp. fresh thyme leaves
1 large egg, lightly beaten
Crawfish Gravy

1. Bring broth and 1 cup water to a boil in a large saucepan. Gradually stir in grits. Cover, reduce heat, and simmer 7 minutes or until thickened, stirring twice. Add ground red pepper and cheese, stirring until cheese melts. Remove from heat.
2. Spoon grits into a greased 13- x 9-inch baking dish. Cover and chill until firm.
3. Preheat oven to 450°. Unmold grits onto a large cutting board, sliding a knife or a spatula under grits to loosen them from dish. Cut grits into ¾-inch cubes. Place cubes in a single layer on a greased large rimmed baking sheet or jelly-roll pan.
4. Bake at 450° for 20 minutes; turn grits cubes, and bake 10 to 12 more minutes or until crisp and browned. Reduce oven temperature to 350°.
5. Meanwhile, heat oil in a large skillet over medium-high heat; add sausage and cook 3 minutes or until browned. Using a slotted spoon, remove sausage from skillet, reserving drippings in pan; drain on paper towels.
6. Reduce heat to medium. Cook celery and next 3 ingredients in hot drippings over medium heat 3 to 4 minutes or until tender. Combine sausage, vegetable mixture, grits cubes, parsley, and thyme in a large bowl. Gradually add egg, stirring gently to coat. Spoon dressing loosely into a greased 13- x 9-inch baking dish.
7. Bake, uncovered, at 350° for 35 minutes or until browned. Serve with Crawfish Gravy.

Crawfish Gravy

Crawfish Gravy

MAKES 4 CUPS
HANDS-ON TIME: 19 MIN.; TOTAL TIME: 19 MIN.

- 6 Tbsp. butter
- 1 lb. cooked, peeled crawfish tails, chopped
- 1 large shallot, minced
- 2 garlic cloves, minced
- ¼ cup all-purpose flour
- 2½ cups chicken broth
- 1 tsp. Cajun seasoning
- 1 bay leaf
- 2 tsp. fresh thyme leaves
- ¼ tsp. freshly ground pepper

1. Melt butter in a large saucepan or Dutch oven over medium-high heat. Add crawfish; sauté 3 to 4 minutes or until browned. Remove crawfish with a slotted spoon, reserving drippings in pan. Sauté shallot and garlic in hot drippings 1 minute or until shallot is tender. Whisk in flour. Reduce heat to medium, and cook 2 minutes or until bubbly and golden brown.

2. Gradually stir in chicken broth. Add Cajun seasoning, bay leaf, thyme, pepper, and crawfish. Bring to a boil; reduce heat, and simmer, uncovered, 7 minutes or until thickened. Remove and discard bay leaf. Serve over Andouille-Cheese Grits Dressing.

Roasted Haricots Verts With Creole Mustard Sauce

MAKES 8 SERVINGS
HANDS-ON TIME: 23 MIN.; TOTAL TIME: 37 MIN.

Slender French green beans are treated with Louisiana flair in this highly rated side.

- 4   (8-oz.) packages trimmed haricots verts or thin green beans
- 2   Tbsp. olive oil
- ¼   tsp. freshly ground pepper
- 3   garlic cloves, thinly sliced
- 4   bacon slices
- ⅔   cup chopped onion
- 2   garlic cloves, minced
- 1½ Tbsp. chopped fresh thyme
- 1½ cups chicken broth
- 2   Tbsp. Creole mustard
- 1   Tbsp. sherry vinegar

1. Preheat oven to 475°. Toss together first 4 ingredients in a large bowl until beans are coated. Spread beans evenly in a single layer in 2 large rimmed baking sheets. Bake at 475° for 14 minutes or until browned.
2. Meanwhile, cook bacon in a large skillet over medium heat 7 to 8 minutes or until crisp; remove bacon, and drain on paper towels, reserving drippings in skillet. Crumble bacon.
3. Sauté onion and garlic in hot drippings 4 minutes or until onion is tender; stir in thyme and broth. Bring to a boil over medium-high heat; boil 5 minutes or until liquid is reduced to 1 cup. Stir in mustard and vinegar; cook 4 minutes or until liquid almost evaporates.
4. Place beans in a large bowl. Pour the sauce over the beans, tossing to coat. Sprinkle with crumbled bacon. Serve hot.

Maque Choux

MAKES 8 SERVINGS
HANDS-ON TIME: 10 MIN.; TOTAL TIME: 34 MIN.

Omitting the whipping cream makes the vegetables in this dish more vibrant. We liked it both ways.

- 10 bacon slices
- 1½ cups chopped onion
- ½   cup coarsely chopped green bell pepper
- ½   cup coarsely chopped red bell pepper
- 2   (16-oz.) packages frozen baby gold and white corn (we tested with Birds Eye)
- 1   Tbsp. Creole seasoning
- 1   cup chicken broth
- 1   cup whipping cream
- 1½ cups grape tomatoes, halved
- ½   cup sliced green onions
-     Garnish: sliced green onions

1. Cook bacon in a large skillet over medium heat 15 minutes or until crisp; remove bacon, and drain on paper towels, reserving 2 Tbsp. drippings in skillet. Crumble bacon.
2. Sauté onion in hot drippings over medium heat 5 minutes or until almost tender. Add bell peppers; sauté 3 minutes or until peppers are almost tender. Stir in crumbled bacon, reserving 2 Tbsp. Stir in corn, Creole seasoning, and broth. Increase heat to medium-high; cook 6 minutes or until corn is tender. Stir in whipping cream, and cook 3 minutes or until creamy and thickened. Stir in tomato and ½ cup green onions. Increase heat to high; cook 2 minutes or just until tomato begins to soften. Sprinkle with reserved bacon, and garnish, if desired.

Sweet Potato Biscuits

MAKES 3 DOZEN
HANDS-ON TIME: 20 MIN.; TOTAL TIME: 32 MIN.

Baking the sweet potato in a hot oven for about 1 hour for these fluffy biscuits creates a sweet, caramelized flavor you won't get if you microwave it.

¾ cup cooked mashed sweet potato (about 1 medium)
½ cup butter, melted
3 Tbsp. light brown sugar
¼ tsp. ground cinnamon
2 cups all-purpose flour
2 tsp. baking powder
1 tsp. salt
½ tsp. baking soda
¾ cup buttermilk

1. Preheat oven to 400°. Combine sweet potato, butter, brown sugar, and cinnamon; beat at medium speed with an electric mixer until blended.

2. Combine flour, baking powder, and salt; stir well. Stir soda into buttermilk. Combine sweet potato mixture, flour mixture, and buttermilk mixture in a large bowl, stirring just until dry ingredients are moistened. Turn dough out onto a lightly floured surface, and knead gently 4 to 6 times.

3. Roll dough to ½-inch thickness; cut with a 1½-inch biscuit cutter. Place on ungreased baking sheets; bake at 400° for 12 to 15 minutes or until golden brown.

'Tis the season of Réveillon, an old French dining tradition that has become a mainstay in New Orleans. Typically it refers to one long dinner or party held on the evening preceding Christmas Day. It comes from the word réveil (meaning "waking") because it involves staying up until dawn.

editor's favorite

Black-and-White Bread Pudding With Bourbon Sauce

MAKES 8 SERVINGS
HANDS-ON TIME: 19 MIN.; TOTAL TIME: 1 HR., 30 MIN.

Soft semi-melted chunks of dark chocolate are nestled inside the pudding, while a bourbon-splashed white chocolate sauce is spooned over each serving.

1 (12-oz.) loaf French bread, cubed and toasted
1 (11.5-oz.) package semisweet chocolate chunks
3 cups milk
1 cup heavy cream
¾ cup sugar
6 oz. white chocolate baking bar, chopped (we tested with Ghirardelli)
4 large eggs, lightly beaten
1 Tbsp. vanilla bean paste
White Chocolate Bourbon Sauce

1. Preheat oven to 350°. Place bread cubes in a buttered 13- x 9-inch baking dish. Sprinkle chocolate chunks over bread.

2. Cook milk, cream, and sugar in a heavy nonaluminum saucepan over medium heat, stirring often, 6 minutes or just until bubbles appear (do not boil); remove from heat. Add white chocolate, stirring until chocolate melts. Gradually stir about one-fourth of hot chocolate mixture into eggs; add egg mixture to remaining hot mixture, stirring constantly. Stir in vanilla bean paste. Pour over bread; let stand 10 minutes.

3. Bake at 350° for 45 minutes or until set. Serve warm with White Chocolate Bourbon Sauce.

White Chocolate Bourbon Sauce

MAKES 1⅓ CUPS
HANDS-ON TIME: 4 MIN.; TOTAL TIME: 6 MIN.

¾ cup heavy cream
6 oz. white chocolate baking bar, chopped
1 Tbsp. butter
⅛ tsp. salt
2 Tbsp. bourbon

1. Cook cream in a heavy nonaluminum saucepan over medium heat, stirring often, 2 minutes or just until bubbles appear (do not boil); remove from heat. Whisk in chocolate, butter, and salt until chocolate melts. Whisk in bourbon.

Both dark and white chocolates take this traditional New Orleans dessert to new heights.

Bananas Foster Cake

MAKES 16 SERVINGS
HANDS-ON TIME: 31 MIN.; TOTAL TIME: 1 HR., 6 MIN.

We loved the glaze for this sweet, moist cake because it contributes all the luscious flavors of traditional Bananas Foster. The cake's also delicious without the glaze.

Cake

- 1 cup butter, softened
- 1 cup granulated sugar
- 1 cup firmly packed light brown sugar
- 5 large eggs
- 3 cups all-purpose flour
- 1 tsp. baking soda
- ¼ tsp. salt
- 1 cup milk
- 3 ripe bananas, mashed
- 1 tsp. vanilla extract
- Cooking spray for baking
- 2 firm ripe bananas, sliced

Brown Sugar Rum Glaze

- 6 Tbsp. light brown sugar
- 1 Tbsp. light corn syrup
- 1 Tbsp. butter
- 2 Tbsp. dark rum
- ¼ tsp. ground cinnamon

Cream Cheese Frosting

- 1 (8-oz.) package cream cheese, softened
- ½ cup butter, softened
- 1 (16-oz.) package powdered sugar, sifted
- 1 Tbsp. milk
- 2 tsp. vanilla extract
- Garnishes: cinnamon sticks, store-bought pralines

1. Prepare cake: Preheat oven to 350°. Beat butter and sugars at medium speed with an electric mixer until fluffy. Add eggs, 1 at a time, beating until blended after each addition.

2. Combine flour, baking soda, and salt; add to butter mixture alternately with milk, beginning and ending with flour mixture. Beat at low speed until blended after each addition, stopping to scrape bowl as needed. Stir in mashed banana and vanilla. Pour batter into 3 (8-inch) round cake pans coated with cooking spray for baking.

3. Bake at 350° for 25 minutes or until a wooden pick inserted in center comes out clean. Run a sharp knife around edges of pan. Cool cake layers in pans on wire racks 5 minutes; remove from pans to wire racks, and cool completely (about 1 hour).

4. Meanwhile, prepare glaze: Bring brown sugar, corn syrup, and 3 Tbsp. water to a boil in a small saucepan, stirring constantly. Cook, stirring constantly, 1 minute or until sugar dissolves. Stir in butter, rum, and cinnamon.

5. Prepare Cream Cheese Frosting: Beat cream cheese and butter at medium speed with an electric mixer until smooth. Gradually add powdered sugar, beating until smooth; stir in milk and vanilla.

6. Pierce cake layers with a wooden pick; drizzle with Brown Sugar Rum Glaze. Let stand for at least 10 minutes.

7. Spread ¼ cup Cream Cheese Frosting on 1 cake layer; arrange half of banana slices over frosting. Repeat procedure with a second cake layer, ¼ cup frosting, and remaining half of banana slices. Top with third cake layer. Frost top and sides of cake with remaining frosting. Garnish, if desired.

Christmas DINNER WITH A TWIST

Not your usual suspects, we've taken holiday classics and given them a new spin—a surprising flavor, an unusual method, or a novel companion. You may never go back to the traditional versions.

menu

CORNBREAD AND SAUSAGE DRESSING-STUFFED MUSHROOMS

PERSIMMON-AND-POMEGRANATE SALAD

PISTACHIO-CRUSTED BEEF WELLINGTON

PAN-ROASTED PORK TENDERLOIN

GARLIC AND GINGER GREEN BEANS

HORSERADISH MASHED POTATOES

ROASTED BABY PUMPKINS WITH JARLSBERG
AND HAZELNUTS

DATE-NUT GALETTE

PUMPKIN PIE WITH CRYSTALLIZED GINGER

serves 6

game plan

up to 1 month ahead:

☐ Prepare crystallized ginger; store in an airtight container.

1 day ahead:

☐ Prepare and chill dressing for salad.

☐ Prepare beef for Pistachio-Crusted Beef Wellington up to Madeira sauce step; cover and chill.

☐ Prepare and marinate pork tenderloin in a large zip-top plastic freezer bag overnight.

☐ Prepare Pumpkin Pie; cover with plastic wrap, and chill overnight.

4 hours ahead:

☐ Prepare filling for stuffed mushrooms; cover and chill.

☐ Cook green beans for Garlic and Ginger Green Beans; plunge in ice water. Place in a large zip-top plastic bag; chill.

☐ Prepare baby pumpkins, but don't bake.

☐ Prepare galette, but don't bake.

☐ Prepare sweetened whipped cream for galette; store in an airtight container in refrigerator.

2 hours ahead:

☐ Prepare and finish Pistachio-Crusted Beef Wellington.

☐ Bake Date-Nut Galette.

1 hour ahead:

☐ Prepare Pan-Roasted Pork Tenderloin.

☐ Prepare Horseradish Mashed Potatoes.

☐ Bake Roasted Baby Pumpkins with Jarlsberg and Hazelnuts.

30 minutes ahead:

•Bake Cornbread and Sausage Dressing-Stuffed Mushrooms.

•Arrange salads on serving plates.

10 minutes ahead:

☐ Finish green beans.

editor's favorite

Cornbread and Sausage Dressing-Stuffed Mushrooms

MAKES 1½ DOZEN
HANDS-ON TIME: 10 MIN.; TOTAL TIME: 41 MIN.

The filling for these mushrooms will remind you of Grandma's turkey dressing, so you can enjoy the taste of the holidays without slaving over a big meal.

18 large fresh mushrooms

5 Tbsp. butter, melted and divided

4 oz. sage-flavored breakfast sausage (we tested with Jimmy Dean)

½ cup finely chopped onion

½ cup finely chopped celery

2 garlic cloves, minced

1½ cups (6 oz.) sharp Cheddar cheese, shredded and divided

1 cup fine cornbread crumbs (about 1 corn muffin)*

1 slice white bread, torn into small pieces

1 large egg, lightly beaten

½ tsp. salt

⅛ tsp. pepper

Garnish: fresh rosemary or other herbs

1. Preheat oven to 400°. Remove and chop mushroom stems. Brush mushroom caps on all sides with 3 Tbsp. butter, and place on a 15- x 10-inch jelly-roll pan.

2. Cook mushroom stems, sausage, and next 3 ingredients in a large skillet over medium-high heat until browned, stirring to crumble sausage. Stir together remaining 2 Tbsp. butter, sausage mixture, 1 cup cheese, cornbread crumbs, and next 4 ingredients in a large bowl. Spoon filling into mushroom caps.

3. Bake at 400° for 15 minutes; top with remaining ½ cup cheese. Bake 5 more minutes or until cheese melts. Garnish platter, if desired.

*You can use a leftover homemade corn muffin or purchase a single muffin from your local bakery or cafeteria.

editor's favorite • quick & easy

Persimmon-and-Pomegranate Salad

MAKES 8 SERVINGS
HANDS-ON TIME: 18 MIN.; TOTAL TIME: 18 MIN.

Choose persimmons that are a deep orange color and that give slightly when gently pressed; otherwise they will be bitter.

- 3 Tbsp. extra virgin olive oil
- 2 Tbsp. honey
- 2 Tbsp. pomegranate juice (we tested with Pom)
- 2 Tbsp. sherry vinegar
- 1 Tbsp. Dijon mustard
- ½ tsp. salt
- ⅛ tsp. freshly ground pepper
- 12 cups sweet baby greens
- 2 ripe Fuyu persimmons, peeled and cut into wedges
- ½ cup pomegranate seeds*
- ½ cup coarsely chopped hazelnuts, toasted

1. Whisk together first 7 ingredients in a small bowl. Divide greens among 8 salad plates; top greens with persimmon slices, and sprinkle with pomegranate seeds. Drizzle dressing over salads, and sprinkle with hazelnuts. Serve immediately.

*Look for pomegranate seeds in the produce department of your supermarket.

editor's favorite • make ahead

Pistachio-Crusted Beef Wellington

MAKES 8 TO 10 SERVINGS
HANDS-ON TIME: 50 MIN.; TOTAL TIME: 2 HR., 19 MIN.

To make this delectable entrée more family friendly and economical, we've substituted duxelles, a rich herbed mushroom mixture, for the traditional pâté. If you're a member of a wholesale club, purchase your tenderloin there to make this holiday splurge even more affordable.

- 1 (4-lb.) beef tenderloin, trimmed
- ¾ tsp. salt, divided
- ¾ tsp. freshly ground pepper, divided
- ¼ cup butter, divided
- 2 Tbsp. olive oil, divided
- ¾ cup Japanese breadcrumbs (panko)
- ½ cup pistachios
- ¼ cup Dijon mustard
- 2 garlic cloves
- 2 large shallots, quartered
- 4 (8-oz.) packages sliced fresh mushrooms
- 1 tsp. fresh thyme leaves
- 1 cup Madeira
- 1 (14-oz.) can beef broth
- 4 tsp. cornstarch
- 20 thin slices prosciutto
- 1 (17.3-oz.) package frozen puff pastry sheets, thawed
- 1 egg yolk

1. Cut tenderloin in half; tuck narrow end under, if necessary, to create an even thickness in each portion. Sprinkle beef with ½ tsp. salt and ½ tsp. pepper.

2. Heat 2 Tbsp. butter and 1 Tbsp. oil in a large skillet over medium-high heat until butter melts. Add beef; cook 3 minutes on each side until browned. Remove from pan; let cool 10 minutes.

3. Meanwhile, process breadcrumbs and pistachios in a food processor until nuts are finely chopped. Place pistachio mixture in a large shallow dish. Brush beef with mustard and dredge in pistachio mixture. Cover and chill 30 minutes.

4. Meanwhile, with processor running, drop garlic through food chute; process until minced. Add shallots; process until chopped. Heat remaining 2 Tbsp. butter and 1 Tbsp. oil in a large skillet over medium heat until butter melts. Add shallot mixture; cook, stirring occasionally, while processing half of mushrooms until finely chopped. Stir chopped mushrooms into shallot mixture. Process remaining half of mushrooms until finely chopped; stir into shallot mixture. Add remaining ¼ tsp. salt, remaining ¼ tsp. pepper, and thyme. Cook 15 minutes or until

liquid evaporates, stirring often. Remove mushroom mixture from pan, and cool to room temperature. Add Madeira and broth to hot pan. Combine cornstarch and 1 Tbsp. water, stirring until smooth. Whisk cornstarch mixture into broth mixture. Cook, whisking constantly, over medium-high heat 1 minute or until thickened. Set aside.

5. On a work surface, overlap a couple of sheets of plastic wrap to create 2 rectangles, long and wide enough to wrap each portion of beef. Overlap 10 prosciutto slices on each plastic wrap rectangle to create a rectangle large enough to completely wrap around 1 prepared beef portion. Spread half of mushroom mixture over each prosciutto rectangle. Place a beef portion on mushroom mixture lengthwise next to a long edge of each rectangle. Using plastic wrap to help, roll up each portion of beef with mushroom-lined prosciutto. Chill 30 minutes.

6. Preheat oven to 425°. Roll each sheet of puff pastry into a 14- x 12-inch rectangle (or large enough to completely wrap 1 prepared beef portion in dough). Carefully unwrap each beef portion and place in center of a dough rectangle. Wrap each portion with dough, pressing to seal. Place wrapped beef, seam side down, on a large lightly greased baking sheet. Using a sharp knife, slash tops of dough in a decorative pattern. (Do not cut completely through dough.)

7. Whisk together egg yolk and 1 tsp. water. Brush dough on all sides with egg wash. Bake at 425° for 50 minutes or until desired degree of doneness, shielding with aluminum foil after 25 to 30 minutes, if necessary, to prevent excessive browning.

8. While beef bakes, reheat Madeira sauce. Let beef stand 10 minutes before slicing. Serve with Madeira sauce.

make ahead:

You can prepare beef through Step 5 up to 1 day ahead.

**Pistachio-Crusted
Beef Wellington**

Let the beef stand 10 minutes before slicing.

Pan-Roasted Pork Tenderloin

MAKES 8 SERVINGS
HANDS-ON TIME: 20 MIN. TOTAL TIME: 8 HR., 57 MIN.

Canned green peppercorns resemble capers. You'll find them with the pickles and olives at your supermarket. Be sure to rinse them before adding to the sauce—they're packed in brine, which would make the sauce too salty.

¼	cup olive oil
2	Tbsp. fresh lemon juice
1	Tbsp. minced fresh thyme
1	tsp. salt
½	tsp. freshly ground pepper
3	garlic cloves, minced
3	(1-lb.) pork tenderloins, trimmed
1	Tbsp. olive oil
2	Tbsp. butter
¼	cup minced shallots
1½	Tbsp. green peppercorns, rinsed and drained
½	cup brandy
¼	cup chicken broth (we tested with Swanson's)
2	cups heavy whipping cream
½	tsp. salt

1. Combine first 6 ingredients in a large zip-top plastic freezer bag. Add pork; seal bag. Marinate in refrigerator 8 hours.

2. Remove pork from marinade, discarding marinade.

3. Heat 1 Tbsp. olive oil in a large nonstick skillet over medium-high heat; add pork. Cook 12 minutes or until browned, turning occasionally. Add ½ cup water to pan, stirring to loosen browned bits. Cover, reduce heat, and simmer 13 minutes or until a meat thermometer inserted in thickest portion registers 155° and liquid has evaporated. Remove pork, reserving drippings in pan; cover loosely with foil. Let stand 10 minutes or until thermometer registers 160°.

4. Add butter to drippings in pan; cook over medium heat until melted. Add shallots and peppercorns; cook 1 minute. Remove pan from heat; add brandy, stirring to loosen brown bits. Carefully ignite the fumes just above mixture with a long match or long multipurpose lighter. Let flames die down. Stir in chicken broth. Bring to a boil; boil 1 minute. Stir in whipping cream. Bring to a boil; reduce heat, and simmer 12 to 14 minutes or until slightly thickened. Stir in ½ tsp. salt.

5. Cut pork diagonally across grain into ½-inch-thick slices. Serve with peppercorn sauce.

Pan-Roasted Pork Tenderloin; Roasted Baby
Pumpkins With Jarlsberg and Hazelnuts;
Garlic and Ginger Green Beans

quick & easy

Garlic and Ginger Green Beans

MAKES 8 SERVINGS
HANDS-ON TIME: 7 MIN.; TOTAL TIME: 19 MIN.

Simple green beans get spruced up with fresh ginger and garlic. When buying ginger, be sure to pick a root that is firm and smooth.

1½ lb. green beans, trimmed
 2 Tbsp. unsalted butter
 1 Tbsp. olive oil
 2 large garlic cloves, minced
 1 Tbsp. grated fresh ginger
 ¾ tsp. salt
 ½ tsp. freshly ground pepper
 3 Tbsp. minced fresh flat-leaf parsley

1. Cook green beans in boiling salted water to cover 7 minutes or until crisp-tender; drain. Plunge beans into a bowl of ice water to stop the cooking process; drain.
2. Heat butter and oil in a large skillet over medium heat; add garlic and ginger, and sauté 1 minute or until golden. Stir in green beans, salt, and pepper; sauté 4 minutes or until beans are thoroughly heated. Sprinkle with parsley just before serving.

Horseradish Mashed Potatoes

MAKES 6 SERVINGS
HANDS-ON TIME: 10 MIN.; TOTAL TIME: 28 MIN.

Microwaving the half-and-half for 1 minute or until very warm before adding it to the cooked potatoes ensures that they will be fluffy when mashed.

 2 lbs. Yukon gold potatoes, peeled and cut into ¾-inch
      cubes
 ¼ cup butter, softened
 ⅔ cup warm half-and-half
1½ Tbsp. prepared horseradish
 1 tsp. salt
 1 tsp. stone-ground mustard
 ½ tsp. freshly ground pepper
 3 green onions, thinly sliced (optional)

1. Cook potatoes in boiling water to cover in a large saucepan 18 minutes or until tender. Drain potatoes, and return to pan. Add butter and next 5 ingredients; mash with a potato masher to desired consistency. Sprinkle with green onions, if desired.

Dress down for dinner. Omit the tablecloth and let the rustic wood of your table contrast with the glisten and shine of refined silver, china, and crystal.

Roasted Baby Pumpkins With Jarlsberg and Hazelnuts

MAKES 8 SERVINGS
HANDS-ON TIME: 23 MIN.; TOTAL TIME: 1 HR., 14 MIN.

Microwaving the pumpkins for a few minutes before removing the tops makes them easier to prepare.

  2   Tbsp. butter
  1   medium onion, chopped
  1   tsp. salt, divided
  ¼   tsp. freshly ground pepper
1¼   cups (6 oz.) shredded Jarlsberg cheese
  ¾   cup chopped hazelnuts, toasted
  1   tsp. hot sauce (we tested with Tabasco)
  8   (8 oz.) baby pumpkins*
  1   cup whipping cream

1. Preheat oven to 350°. Melt butter in a medium nonstick skillet over medium-high heat. Add onion, ½ tsp. salt, and pepper; cook 3 minutes or until tender, stirring often. Place onion mixture in a medium bowl. Stir in cheese, hazelnuts, and hot sauce.

2. Pierce pumpkins several times with a small sharp knife. Microwave at HIGH 6 minutes. Cut tops off pumpkins, reserving tops; remove and discard seeds. Sprinkle insides of pumpkins with remaining ½ teaspoon salt. Spoon cheese mixture into pumpkins; top evenly with cream, and replace tops. Place pumpkins on a baking sheet coated with cooking spray.

3. Bake at 350° for 45 minutes or until pumpkins are tender.

*You may substitute 4 (1 lb.) acorn squash for the pumpkins. Preheat oven to 350°. Pierce squash; microwave at HIGH 8 minutes. Cut in half vertically; remove and discard seeds. Spoon cheese mixture into squash halves; place on a large rimmed baking sheet. Cover with aluminum foil, and bake at 350° for 1 hour or until squash are tender.

If you prefer, substitute acorn squash for pumpkins in this recipe.

Date-Nut Galette

MAKES 8 SERVINGS
HANDS-ON TIME: 16 MIN.; TOTAL TIME: 1 HR., 1 MIN.

Make a quick-and-easy crème anglaise for this dessert by simply melting a rich French vanilla ice cream and drizzling it over each serving, if desired.

1 (15-oz.) package refrigerated piecrusts
Parchment paper
2 large eggs
⅓ cup dark corn syrup
2 Tbsp. butter, melted
1 tsp. vanilla extract
1 tsp. orange zest
¼ tsp. salt
1 cup chopped walnuts
1 (8-oz.) package chopped dates
1 egg white
Sweetened whipped cream
Garnish: orange zest strips

1. Preheat oven to 425°. Unroll 1 piecrust, and place on a parchment paper-lined baking sheet; lightly brush top of crust with water. Unroll remaining crust; place over bottom crust. Gently roll or press crusts together to form a 12-inch circle.

2. Whisk together eggs and next 5 ingredients; stir in walnuts and dates. Spoon date filling into center of prepared crust, spreading to within 2 inches of edges. Fold a 2-inch border of dough over filling, overlapping edges. Whisk together egg white and 1 tsp. water in a small bowl. Brush border of dough with egg white mixture.

3. Bake on lowest oven rack at 425° for 10 minutes. Reduce oven temperature to 350°, and bake 35 minutes or until pastry is browned. Cool on a wire rack before serving with dollops of sweetened whipped cream. Garnish, if desired.

editor's favorite • make ahead

Pumpkin Pie With Crystallized Ginger

MAKES 1 (9-INCH) PIE
HANDS-ON TIME: 11 MIN.; TOTAL TIME: 3 HR., 49 MIN.

Crystallized Ginger
½ (15-oz.) package refrigerated piecrusts
3 large eggs
1 (15-oz.) can pumpkin
1 tsp. pumpkin pie spice
1 tsp. vanilla extract
1 cup half-and-half
Sweetened whipped cream

1. Prepare Crystallized Ginger, reserving excess sugar.
2. Preheat oven to 425°. Fit piecrust into a 9-inch pie plate according to package directions; fold edges under, and crimp. Chill until ready to use.
3. Whisk eggs and 1 cup reserved excess sugar together in a large bowl; whisk in pumpkin, pumpkin pie spice, and vanilla. Gradually whisk in half-and-half. Pour filling into prepared piecrust.
4. Bake at 425° for 15 minutes. Reduce oven temperature to 350°; bake 38 more minutes or until set. Cool completely on a wire rack. Chill at least 2 hours. Serve with dollops of sweetened whipped cream and a generous sprinkling of Crystallized Ginger.

editor's favorite • great gift • make ahead

Crystallized Ginger

MAKES 1½ CUPS

Sprinkle chopped Crystallized Ginger on stewed fruit, stir into muffin or cake batter, or dip slices in dark chocolate to accompany espresso.

½ lb. fresh ginger, peeled and cut into ⅛-inch slices (about 1¾ cups)
2 cups sugar, divided

1. Cook ginger in boiling water to cover 20 minutes or until tender; drain and let dry on a wire rack.
2. Combine ginger, 1 cup sugar, and 2 Tbsp. water in a 12-inch skillet. Cook, uncovered, over medium-low heat 52 minutes or until thick, syrupy, and beginning to crystallize, stirring occasionally to separate slices. (Do not let sugar caramelize.) Using a slotted spoon, transfer ginger to a wire rack set over paper towels. Cool completely.
3. Place remaining 1 cup sugar in a large bowl. Add ginger slices, tossing to coat. Spoon sugared ginger into a wire-mesh sieve; shake excess sugar back into bowl, and reserve for other uses in place of regular sugar. Store Crystallized Ginger and excess sugar in airtight containers up to 1 month.

Package Crystallized Ginger in cellophane bags tied with ribbon to give as gifts.

Sparkling Cosmopolitan

New Year's Eve
DESSERT PARTY

Resolve to get the New Year off to a sweet start with a decadent menu of inspired cocktails and confectionary delights.

menu

Sparkling Cosmopolitan

Pom-Apple-Grape Mocktail

Vanilla Coffee

White Chocolate-Key Lime
Cheesecake Squares

Petite Persimmon Puffs

Cranberry Pistachio Tartlets

Chocolate Brown Sugar Cake
With Caramel Filling and
Pecan Florentine

serves 16

game plan

1 week ahead:

- ☐ Prepare Vanilla Bean Syrup.
- ☐ Prepare and bake tart shells for Cranberry Pistachio Tartlets; place in zip-top plastic freezer bags. Seal and freeze.

2 days ahead:

- ☐ Prepare White Chocolate-Key Lime Cheesecake Squares; cover loosely with plastic wrap and chill.
- ☐ Prepare persimmon filling; cover and chill.
- ☐ Make cake layers, wrap in plastic wrap, and refrigerate.

1 day ahead:

- ☐ Combine and chill ingredients for Sparkling Cosmopolitan except for sparkling wine.
- ☐ Prepare garnish for Sparkling Cosmopolitan.
- ☐ Bake puff pastry cups; cool and store in an airtight container.
- ☐ Make Pecan Florentine, Caramel Filling, and frosting for cake. Assemble cake, except for garnish, cover loosely with plastic wrap, and chill.

4 hours ahead:

- ☐ Prepare Cranberry Pistachio Tartlets.

1 to 2 hours ahead:

- ☐ Assemble Petite Persimmon Puffs.
- ☐ Garnish Chocolate Brown Sugar Cake.

30 minutes ahead:

- ☐ Set up coffee bar.

10 minutes ahead:

- ☐ Brew coffee.

---

editor's favorite • quick & easy

Sparkling Cosmopolitan

MAKES 16 SERVINGS
HANDS-ON TIME: 3 MIN.; TOTAL TIME: 3 MIN.

Traditional cosmopolitans get a face-lift with the addition of bubbly Champagne—we suggest having a few extra bottles on hand for guests who prefer a higher ratio of Champagne to cranberry mixture.

- 3 cups cranberry juice
- 1 cup vodka
- 1 cup triple sec
- ⅓ cup fresh lime juice
- 2 (750-ml.) bottles sparkling wine or Champagne
- Garnish: sugared cranberries*

1. Stir together first 4 ingredients in a large pitcher. Chill until ready to serve.
2. Pour about ⅓ cup cranberry mixture into each of 16 champagne glasses. Fill each glass with sparkling wine. Garnish, if desired.

*Roll fresh cranberries in light corn syrup; remove from syrup with a fork, shaking off excess. Dredge in sugar, and let dry on a wire rack. Thread several sugared cranberries on a wooden pick, and place in each glass.

quick & easy

Pom-Apple-Grape Mocktail

MAKES 6 SERVINGS
HANDS-ON TIME: 3 MIN.; TOTAL TIME: 3 MIN.

The flavors of both the sparkling apple cider and the white grape juice in this nonalcoholic refresher were great, but we preferred the clarity of the apple cider.

- 2 cups sparkling apple cider* or white grape juice, chilled
- ½ cup pomegranate juice*, chilled
- Pomegranate seeds

1. Pour ⅓ cup cider or grape juice in each of 6 champagne glasses. Divide pomegranate juice among the glasses. Drop a few pomegranate seeds in each glass. Serve immediately.

*We tested with Martinelli's Sparkling Apple Cider and Pom pomegranate juice.

Vanilla Coffee

Vanilla Coffee

MAKES 1 SERVING
HANDS-ON TIME: 2 MIN.; TOTAL TIME: 10 MIN.

Vanilla Bean Syrup is a delightful alternative to sugar to sweeten after-dinner coffee. Make your coffee bar a festive affair by offering whipped topping and a variety of flavorings, sweeteners, creamers, and spirits.

Vanilla Bean Syrup
1 cup hot brewed coffee
Half-and-half
1 Tbsp. vanilla-flavored vodka (optional)
Shaved bittersweet chocolate

1. Stir 1 Tbsp., or desired amount, of Vanilla Bean Syrup into hot coffee. Stir in desired amount of half-and-half and vanilla vodka, if desired. Sprinkle with shaved bittersweet chocolate.

Vanilla Bean Syrup

MAKES 2½ CUPS
HANDS-ON TIME: 2 MIN.; TOTAL TIME: 8 MIN.

2 cups sugar
1 vanilla bean, split lengthwise

1. Combine 2 cups water and sugar in a medium saucepan; cook over medium heat until sugar dissolves, stirring frequently. Scrape vanilla bean seeds into sugar syrup; add vanilla bean pod to syrup. Remove from heat, and let cool completely. Remove and discard vanilla bean pod.

make ahead:

Prepare Vanilla Bean Syrup up to 1 week ahead. Cover and store in the refrigerator.

make ahead

White Chocolate-Key Lime Cheesecake Squares

MAKES 16 SQUARES
HANDS-ON TIME: 28 MIN.; TOTAL TIME: 1 HR., 57 MIN.

Velvety white chocolate and tart Key lime are paired together in these luscious squares.

½ cup butter, softened
¼ cup firmly packed light brown sugar
1 tsp. vanilla extract
1 cup all-purpose flour
1 (8-oz.) package cream cheese, softened
1½ cups powdered sugar
1 large egg
1 tsp. lime zest
1 tsp. vanilla extract
3 oz. white chocolate, melted
4 large egg yolks
¾ cup sugar
1 Tbsp. cornstarch
¼ cup bottled Key lime juice
2 tsp. lime zest
2 Tbsp. butter
Garnish: lime slices

1. Preheat oven to 325°. Beat first 2 ingredients at medium speed with an electric mixer until creamy; add 1 tsp. vanilla, beating until blended. Add flour; beat at low speed until blended. Press dough into a lightly greased 8-inch square pan. Bake at 325° for 25 minutes or until golden brown. Let cool on a wire rack.
2. While crust bakes, beat cream cheese and powdered sugar at medium speed until creamy. Add egg, 1 tsp. lime zest, and 1 tsp. vanilla; beat well. Add melted white chocolate; beat until combined. Cover and chill filling.
3. While cream cheese filling chills, make lime curd. Combine egg yolks, ¾ cup sugar, and cornstarch in a medium saucepan; gradually stir in ¾ cup water and lime juice. Cook over medium-low heat, stirring constantly, until mixture thickens and coats the back of a metal spoon. Remove from heat; stir in 2 tsp. lime zest and 2 Tbsp. butter. Remove from heat, and let cool 10 minutes.
4. Spread chilled cream cheese filling over cooled crust. Pour lime curd over cream cheese filling. Bake at 325° for 40 minutes or until edges are lightly browned. Let cool completely on a wire rack. Cut into squares. Garnish with lime slices, if desired. Store in refrigerator.

editor's favorite • make ahead

Petite Persimmon Puffs

MAKES 3 DOZEN
HANDS-ON TIME: 55 MIN.; TOTAL TIME: 1 HR., 35 MIN.

½ (17.3-oz.) package frozen puff pastry sheets, thawed
1 egg white, lightly beaten
1 Tbsp. turbinado sugar
3 Fuyu persimmons, peeled and chopped (about ¾ pound)*
3 Tbsp. apricot preserves
2 tsp. sugar
2 tsp. butter
2 tsp. honey
Powdered sugar

1. Preheat oven to 400°. Unfold puff pastry sheet; roll into an 11-inch square. Cut into 36 squares. Place each puff pastry square in lightly greased miniature muffin cups. Press each square gently into cups, letting corners extend slightly over edges of cups. Lightly brush each pastry cup with egg white, and sprinkle turbinado sugar on corners of pastry.
2. Bake at 400° for 10 minutes or until lightly puffed and golden. Remove from oven; immediately press the end of the handle of a wooden spoon into center of each cup to form a hole. Remove puff pastry cups from muffin pans; cool completely on a wire rack.
3. Meanwhile, combine persimmons and next 4 ingredients in a medium saucepan. Bring to a boil, reduce heat, and simmer 20 minutes or until persimmons are very soft, stirring occasionally. Mash persimmon mixture with a potato masher until consistency of fruit jam. Cover and chill 30 minutes.
4. Spoon about ½ tsp. persimmon filling into each puff pastry shell; sprinkle each shell with powdered sugar.

*Fuyu persimmons are a nonastringent persimmon variety and the best choice for these delicate morsels because they won't surprise you with a bitter experience should you select fruit that isn't perfectly ripe. They can be eaten when very firm or very soft, but we preferred fruit that had a slight "give" when lightly pressed.

make ahead:

Bake puff pastry cups up to 1 day ahead; cool completely and store in an airtight container. Persimmon filling may also be made up to 2 days ahead and stored, covered, in the refrigerator.

White Chocolate-Key Lime
Cheesecake Squares and
Petite Persimmon Puffs

editor's favorite • make ahead

Cranberry Pistachio Tartlets

MAKES 2 DOZEN
HANDS-ON TIME: 12 MIN.; TOTAL TIME: 1 HR., 10 MIN.

The filling for these tiny pies is similar to that of pecan pie with a chewy, nutty topping of cranberries and pistachios.

Pistachio Pastry Shells

⅓ cup butter, softened
1 (3-oz.) package cream cheese, softened
1 cup all-purpose flour
⅓ cup finely chopped pistachios
2 Tbsp. powdered sugar

Cranberry Pistachio Filling

2 large eggs
⅔ cup sugar
⅓ cup light corn syrup
2 Tbsp. butter, melted
1 tsp. vanilla extract
⅓ cup coarsely chopped sweetened dried cranberries
   (we tested with Craisins)
⅓ cup chopped pistachios

Garnish: Sweetened whipped cream, finely chopped pistachios, and chopped sweetened dried cranberries

1. Prepare Pistachio Pastry Shells: Beat butter and cream cheese at medium speed with an electric mixer until smooth. Add flour, pistachios, and powdered sugar, beating well. Shape dough into a ball; wrap in wax paper, and chill 1 hour.
2. Divide dough into 24 balls. Place balls in 2 lightly greased (12-cup) miniature muffin pans. Press balls into bottom and up sides of pans. Chill until ready to fill.
3. Prepare Cranberry Pistachio Filling: Preheat oven to 350°. Whisk eggs in a medium bowl; whisk in sugar and next 3 ingredients. Add cranberries and pistachios, stirring well.
4. Remove pastry shells from refrigerator. Spoon filling into shells. Bake at 350° for 24 minutes or just until set. Let cool in pans 5 minutes. Remove from pans, and cool completely on wire racks. Garnish, if desired.

make ahead:

Prepare, bake, and cool tartlets. Carefully place in zip-top plastic freezer bags; seal bags, and freeze up to 1 week. Thaw at room temperature.

Miniature muffin pans are the perfect size for these tasty tartlets.

editor's favorite • make ahead

Chocolate Brown Sugar Cake With Caramel Filling and Pecan Florentine

MAKES 16 SERVINGS
HANDS-ON TIME: 1 HR.; TOTAL TIME: 1 HR., 15 MIN.

This showstopper is as decadent as it is stunning. It offers the whole dessert package: moist, chocolaty layers; gooey caramel filling; soft swirls of rich frosting; all topped with delicate, crunchy Pecan Florentine.

Cake

½ cup butter, softened
2 cups firmly packed light brown sugar
3 large eggs
1 tsp. vanilla extract
2 (1-oz.) squares unsweetened chocolate, melted
2¼ cups all-purpose flour
1 tsp. baking soda
½ tsp. salt
1 cup buttermilk
   Cooking spray for baking

Pecan Florentine

6 Tbsp. sugar
6 Tbsp. heavy cream
2 Tbsp. butter
1 Tbsp. all-purpose flour
1½ cups finely chopped pecans
   Parchment paper

Caramel Filling

1 cup firmly packed light brown sugar
3 Tbsp. all-purpose flour
1 cup evaporated milk
2 egg yolks, lightly beaten
2 Tbsp. butter, softened

Chocolate Buttercream Frosting

½ cup semisweet chocolate morsels
½ cup milk, divided
¾ cup butter, softened
2 tsp. vanilla extract
5 cups powdered sugar
¾ cup unsweetened cocoa
¼ tsp. salt

1. Prepare cake: Preheat oven to 350°. Beat butter at medium speed with an electric mixer until creamy; gradually add sugar, beating well. Add eggs, 1 at a time, beating until blended after each addition. Stir in vanilla and chocolate.

2. Combine flour, baking soda, and salt; add to butter mixture alternately with buttermilk, beginning and ending with flour mixture. Beat at low speed until blended after each addition, stopping to scrape bowl as needed.

3. Pour batter into 2 (8-inch) square cake pans coated with cooking spray for baking. Bake at 350° for 25 to 30 minutes or until a wooden pick inserted in center comes out clean. Cool in pans on wire racks 5 minutes; remove from pans to wire racks, and cool completely (about 1 hour).

4. Meanwhile, prepare Pecan Florentine: Preheat oven to 300°. Combine first 3 ingredients in a small saucepan; bring to a boil over medium-high heat. Remove from heat, and stir in flour and pecans. Pour onto a parchment paper-lined baking sheet, pressing into a single layer using the back of a spoon. Bake at 300° for 28 minutes or until bubbly and golden. Cool on pan 10 minutes. Cut into desired shapes with a pizza cutter, or break into shards. Cool completely.

5. Meanwhile, prepare Caramel Filling: Combine sugar and flour in a small saucepan; gradually whisk in evaporated milk. Bring to a boil over medium heat, whisking constantly. Boil, whisking constantly, 1 minute; remove from heat. Gradually whisk about one-fourth of hot mixture into egg yolks, whisking constantly; add yolk mixture to remaining hot caramel mixture, whisking constantly. Cook over medium heat 1 minute, whisking constantly. Remove from heat; whisk in butter until melted. Cool completely.

6. Prepare Chocolate Buttercream Frosting: Combine chocolate morsels and ¼ cup milk in a small saucepan; cook over low heat, stirring often until smooth. Remove from heat; cool to room temperature.

7. Beat butter at low speed with a heavy-duty stand mixer until creamy; gradually add chocolate mixture, beating until smooth. Add remaining ¼ cup milk, vanilla, and remaining ingredients; beat until smooth.

8. Spread Caramel Filling between cake layers; reserve ¼ cup for garnish.

9. Spread Chocolate Buttercream Frosting on top and sides of cake. Garnish with reserved Caramel Filling and desired amount of Pecan Florentine. Serve any remaining Pecan Florentine as snacks.

make ahead:

Fill and frost cake and prepare Pecan Florentine 1 day ahead. Garnish with reserved Caramel Filling and Pecan Florentine before serving.

festive
DECORATIONS

Welcome the season with a home filled with fresh greenery and
do-it-yourself trimmings. Dozens of colorful photos show
you how simple it can be.

decorate with
WREATHS

Nothing says Christmas like a wreath. Hang one on the front door and another above the mantel to fill your home with holiday magic. On these pages, you'll find lots of fresh ideas for this seasonal favorite.

Magnolia leaves make perfect holiday wreaths. They dry beautifully, transitioning from green to a lovely bronzy gold.

To make a magnolia wreath, start with a florist foam wreath, which can be found at most crafts and discount stores. Soak the wreath in water. Insert individual magnolia leaves into the foam so they are perpendicular to the form, covering the entire wreath. To hang the wreath, loop ribbon around the top of the wreath, and secure the ribbon with a tack or small finishing nail. Use florist wire to attach a bow.

Fresh magnolia wreaths will last two to three weeks. You can refresh the greenery by soaking the entire wreath in a tub of water for a few minutes.

Personalize your wreath with a variety of nontraditional trims. Strands of Spanish moss add unexpected flair to a pine wreath *(left)*, while a small owl and bird's nest seem comfortably at home on a shaggy cypress wreath *(right)*.

Versatile grapevine wreaths make ideal bases for berries. For the trio of wreaths shown below, stems of nandina, popcorn (Chinese tallow), and privet berries are simply wedged into the wreaths.

The scent of fresh citrus blends beautifully with aromatic evergreens, and the contrast of brilliant orange against dark green provides a stunning seasonal display.

To attach fruit to a greenery wreath or garland, insert a wired florist pick into the fruit, and then wire in place. Use loose oranges *(as seen in the galvanized buckets shown at right)* to carry pops of color throughout the decoration.

super citrusy scents:

☐ To maximize the release of citrusy fragrance, use a sharp knife to make vertical slits in the rind.

☐ Allow the slit oranges to air-dry for a few hours before attaching them to allow time for the juice to begin to dry.

☐ Using wired florist picks, attach the oranges to a wreath *(as shown on the seeded eucalyptus wreath below)*, or arrange several in a glass bowl for a festive potpourri. The lovely aroma will linger for days.

☐ Dress up arrangements of oranges and greenery with gold- or copper-colored ribbons to boost the festive mood.

Wreaths that break the round barrier garner even more attention than their circular cousins. Add to that an unusual hanging technique, such as two ribbon hangers instead of one *(left)*, or unique embellishments, such as flattened flatware stamped with seasonal sentiments *(opposite and below)*, and your holiday decorating takes a giant ornamental leap. To make a square wreath, tape blocks of florist foam to a wooden picture frame, then insert flowers or evergreen sprigs.

Use sheer ribbons to tie decorations to wreaths, trees, and garlands for a more decorative punch.

Coordinate wreath colors to suit your room's decor. Tie brightly colored ribbons into bows and wire them to an evergreen wreath to complement the room's color scheme (*above and right*). For added interest, use a mix of ribbon textures, widths, and compatible colors.

Take advantage of a bright wall color, such as the red wall shown on the opposite page, to showcase a frosty white pinecone wreath. Hang wreaths in front of mirrors to double their impact.

make your
MANTEL MERRY

As the natural focal point in a room, the mantel becomes the perfect stage for creating holiday drama using your favorite finery.

* *

With just a few favorite pieces you can create a dazzling mantel display. If your room has a high ceiling, start with one or two oversized pieces, such as the tall candelabra shown on the opposite page. Arrange other pieces with a similar color scheme along the mantel. Here, mercury glass trees, a silver beaded garland, votive holders, and ribbons share a silvery tone. For your arrangement, introduce a unifying element like the wispy cedar clippings that are tucked around the bases of the trees and candelabra. Carry elements of the decoration to the coffee table and other areas of the room.

* *

Let unique pieces set the mantel's mood. On this page, silver trays with chalkboard surfaces suitable for personalizing command attention and offer a creative way to identify stockings. Vivid red berries, candles, and tiny packages add the perfect color complement to the silver.

Vintage-themed wall hangings (*opposite*) establish a retro look that's carried out on the mantel with mid-century tinsel trees and figurines.

Add abundance with a refreshing array of clear glass vases filled with fresh flowers, berries, candy canes, and Christmassy evergreen clippings. For a long-lasting arrangement, try this versatile setup using only greenery sprigs and berries. Change the water every few days to keep the clippings fresh.

Southern symbols of the season gather for a colorfully fresh mantel decoration. The simple arrangement of pineapples, magnolia leaves, and fresh fruits is an updated expression of the traditional Williamsburg look.

When using small objects on the mantel, such as fruit, be sure to elevate some of the pieces to give more visual appeal *(above)*.

For the pineapple arrangement, set a pineapple atop moistened florist foam. Insert florist picks into fruit, and push them into the foam around the pineapple. Fill in with leaves and berries *(right)*.

Imagination rules when it comes to innovative holiday designs. A cherub swings above the mantel, secured by a garland attached to the ceiling *(right)*.

Red poinsettias explode from silver galvanized buckets nestled in a swath of burlap *(opposite)*.

Drinking glasses do double duty as candleholders *(below)*. Silver and gold beads in the glasses add sparkle. For upside-down glasses, fill an upright glass with beads, put a piece of cardboard over the top, and flip the glass over.

Glorious greenery abounds on a white mantel. For this arrangement, cover the mantel with plastic, such as a large garbage bag, and then place trays filled with water-soaked florist foam on the plastic. Insert an assortment of greenery into the florist foam, and accent with stems of fresh flowers, if desired.

set a CHEERY TABLE

Complete the setting for your holiday meals with a table that echoes the special occasion. On these pages, you'll find a medley of styles to suit the mood—from no-frills elegance to casual whimsey.

Rustically sophisticated, a birch-bark container filled with seeded eucalyptus and calla lilies is an easygoing decoration that's just right for everyday gatherings *(below)*. When setting a more festive table, remember to add votive candles for de rigueur holiday twinkle.

A metal angel and lilies anchored in frogs give height to a dining table *(opposite)*. Shorter iron pillar holders fill in holes to create a pleasing balance. Simple yet grand, the spacing of this arrangement allows for good visibility across the table.

Little wreaths make a big statement when showcased in square glass vases. The wreaths shown here are made by wiring stems of rosemary into circles. To hang them, knot a length of ribbon around each wreath, slip a long cinnamon stick through the loop, and lay the stick across the top of a vase. Group several vases on a tray or platter for a pretty centerpiece that will last for several days.

Think in terms of groupings when planning a seasonal centerpiece. At Christmas, it's true— more is merrier!

Multiples go a long way in styling a successful centerpiece. For the fruit and flower arrangement below, place moistened florist foam on a tray. Set pillar candles on top of the foam, then stick stems of flowers, berries, and greenery into the foam. Use florist picks to secure the fruit into the foam.

The displays on the opposite page show the impact of multiplication. Similar objects repeated in a grouping enrich the effect.

* * * * * * * * * * * * * * * * * * * *

December is the month for going over the top—so look up when you're setting the table. Drape icicle lights from the ceiling *(right)* to mimic a snowy sky above a carnation snowman; fill the chandelier with baby's breath, and add tall, painted branches to bring attention upward *(below)*; or swag windows with abundant garlands so the whole room gets in the jolly mood.

* * * * * * * * * * * * * * * * * * * *

trim a TERRIFIC TREE

Sometimes it's fun to shake up the status quo and go for a completely different take on the holiday tree. Here's some inspiration . . .

Use earth-toned ornaments, long pheasant feathers, and chocolate-colored ribbons for a refined, woodsy look *(far left)*. Attach paper butterflies to the branches using florist wire for a bright punch of color *(left)*. Go for timeless appeal with clear glass balls that catch the light's sparkle. Accent the tree with red-wrapped packages tied with white ribbons *(above)*. Create an au naturel tree by trimming it with birds' nests, berries, pinecones, and branches used in place of a tree topper *(right)*.

Given the right trimmings, even a bare branch tree can undergo a magical transformation.

A bare branch tree is just the size for a bedroom. For the grown-ups' tree, wire water vials filled with flowers to the branches *(below)*. For the kids' version, loop a paper-chain garland over the limbs *(opposite, top)*.

If space is tight, select a small evergreen conifer from the local nursery *(opposite, bottom)*. Place it in a suitable container, and trim it in holiday finery. After Christmas, give it a permanent home outside.

For a completely pulled-together look, repeat colors and elements from your tree decorations throughout the room. Here, oversized red bows show up at the top of the tree, on the mantel, and on the table. Red-and-green garlands trail along the mantel and table. Boughs of greenery mirror the evergreen tree.

Use similar decorating elements throughout the room to achieve the maximum "wow" factor.

go NATURAL

Nothing tops the fragrance of fresh greenery and flowers at Christmas.

The crisp partnership of white blooms and varied shades of green suggest a snowy setting. Pair the combo with silver to convey a joyful attitude. To keep your floral budget in check, consider potted flowers, such as orchids, and inexpensive flowers, such as carnations.

Clip greenery from your yard to fill containers. Add stems of white flowers to the greenery arrangements for special gatherings.

* *

Use evergreen and vine wreaths to show-case your favorite ornaments. These "Twelve Days of Christmas" renditions are wired to wreaths and tied to the stair rail with ribbons. Try this technique to display other types of decorations, such as large teardrop-style ornaments or even small framed photos. Hanging several wreaths makes the display more eye-catching.

* *

Branch out and bring your favorite backyard greenery indoors for the holidays. Look for unusual options, such as ivy and smilax.

Ivy and elaeagnus create a natural canopy on a bed, ensuring visions of sugarplums *(below, left)*. Even before Santa arrives, fill stockings with fresh materials, such as seeded eucalyptus and hypericum berries. Tuck in stems of amaryllis in water vials for cheery color *(below)*. Weave an evergreen vine, such as smilax, along the staircase. The smilax vine will stay fresh looking for about a week *(right)*.

This moss-ball chandelier (*opposite*) doesn't provide much light, but you have to admit, it's a bright idea. Invert a wire basket and hang it from a ribbon attached to the ceiling. Use ribbons to tie moss balls to the basket. Wire greenery and berries to the basket, covering the top.

Filling a container with fresh materials is a simple way to add festive decor (*above*). Scout your cabinets for interesting boxes and bowls. For some extra sparkle, nestle a string of lights among the natural materials (*left*).

Celebrate the outdoors with decorations made from natural materials.

* *

Any surface offers an opportunity for
seasonal cheer. Lay evergreen branches on a
tabletop, then layer on other naturals, such
as pinecones, berry stems, and Spanish moss.
Add color with ornaments, candy canes,
and bright citrus fruits. Be sure to cover the
tabletop to protect the surface from scratches
and plant sap. Hide the edges of the covering
beneath the greenery.

* *

Great
RECIPES

This collection of all-new recipes will inspire
you to start your holiday cooking and baking
right away. These versatile dishes are sure
to become year-round favorites.

Breakfast & Brunch FAVORITES

Select from these recipes to plan a hearty early morning feast to enjoy while unwrapping gifts on Christmas morning.

Eggs Benedict Casserole

editor's favorite

Breakfast Soufflés Lorraine

MAKES 6 SERVINGS
HANDS-ON TIME: 30 MIN.; TOTAL TIME: 1 HR., 5 MIN.

Serve your choice of flavor of these soufflés inspired by a famous bakery specialty with piping hot cups of coffee.

    3 bacon slices
    ¾ cup chopped onion
    2 large eggs
 1¼   cups half-and-half
    ⅛ tsp. salt
    ⅛ tsp. freshly ground nutmeg
    ¼ tsp. freshly ground pepper
       Butter-flavored cooking spray
       Parchment paper
    1 (8-oz.) can crescent roll dough (we tested with Pillsbury)
    1 cup (4 oz.) shredded Gruyère cheese

1. Preheat oven to 375°. Cook bacon in a large nonstick skillet over medium-high heat 5 to 7 minutes or until crisp; remove bacon, and drain on paper towels, reserving drippings in skillet. Crumble bacon. Add onion to drippings in skillet; sauté over medium-high heat 5 to 7 minutes or until tender.

2. While onion cooks, whisk eggs until frothy in a bowl; whisk in half-and-half and next 3 ingredients.

3. Set 6 (4½-inch) quiche dishes coated with cooking spray on a large parchment-lined baking sheet. Unroll dough on work surface; roll into a 14- x 12-inch rectangle, sealing perforations. Cut dough into 6 (6- x 4¾-inch) rectangles; press 1 rectangle in bottom and up sides of each prepared dish, letting corners of dough extend over edges. Sprinkle dough with bacon, onion, and cheese. Ladle egg mixture over onion mixture. Carefully fold corners of dough in toward centers over filling, creating an X pattern. (Some egg mixture may seep around edges of dough.) Coat tops with cooking spray.

4. Bake at 375° on bottom shelf for 25 minutes or just until custard is puffed and crust is browned. (Do not overbake.) Let stand 10 minutes before serving.

Fiesta Breakfast Soufflés: Bake 18 frozen crisp potato tot crowns (we tested with Ore-Ida Crispy Crowns) according to package directions. Cook and crumble bacon as directed in recipe, discarding drippings. Omit onion. Prepare egg mixture and crusts as directed, omitting pepper and nutmeg, and adding ½ tsp. adobo sauce from canned chipotle chiles in adobo sauce and ¼ tsp. ground cumin to egg mixture. Omit Gruyère cheese. Divide tots, bacon, 3 Tbsp. thinly sliced green onions, 1 (4-oz.) can drained chopped green chiles, and 1 cup (4 oz.) shredded Mexican four-cheese blend among prepared crusts. Ladle egg mixture over cheese. Fold corners of dough over custard. Coat tops with cooking spray; bake and let stand as directed. Top with salsa, sour cream, and chopped fresh cilantro.

Florentine Breakfast Soufflés: Omit bacon and onion. Sauté 2 garlic cloves, minced, in 2 tsp. olive oil in a large nonstick skillet over medium-high heat 30 seconds. Add 3 Tbsp. drained, chopped bottled roasted red peppers; sauté 30 seconds. Add ¼ cup dry white wine and ¼ cup sliced green onions; cook 1 minute or until wine is almost evaporated. Add 1½ cups coarsely chopped fresh baby spinach; sauté 1 minute or just until spinach wilts. Remove from heat. Prepare egg mixture and crusts as directed, adding ½ tsp. Italian seasoning to egg mixture. Divide spinach mixture among prepared crusts. Omit Gruyère cheese. Ladle egg mixture over spinach mixture; sprinkle tops with ⅓ cup grated Parmesan cheese. Fold corners of dough over custard. Coat tops with cooking spray; bake and let stand as directed. Serve with warm marinara sauce, if desired

editor's favorite • make ahead

Christmas Morning Baked Cheese Grits
(pictured on page 126)

MAKES 8 SERVINGS
HANDS-ON TIME: 15 MIN.; TOTAL TIME: 9 HR., 40 MIN.

This rich casserole has a light and airy texture that melts in your mouth.

1½   cups whipping cream
 ½   tsp. salt
 1   cup uncooked quick-cooking grits
 3   large eggs, lightly beaten
1½   cups (6 oz.) shredded sharp Cheddar cheese
 2   Tbsp. butter
 ⅛   tsp. garlic powder

1. Combine 1½ cups water, whipping cream, and salt in a large saucepan; bring to a boil. Gradually stir in grits. Cover, reduce heat, and simmer 5 minutes, stirring occasionally. Stir in eggs and remaining ingredients.
2. Pour grits mixture into a lightly greased 11- x 7-inch baking dish. Cover and chill at least 8 hours.
3. Remove casserole from refrigerator, and let stand 30 minutes.
4. Meanwhile, preheat oven to 350°. Bake at 350° for 40 minutes or until set and lightly browned. Let stand 5 minutes before serving.

fix it faster:
Preheat oven to 350°. Prepare casserole, but do not chill. Bake at 350° for 40 to 45 minutes or until lightly browned.

editor's favorite • quick & easy

Cinnamon Apple-Stuffed French Toast With Caramel Syrup
(pictured on page 126)

MAKES 8 SERVINGS
HANDS-ON TIME: 24 MIN.; TOTAL TIME: 30 MIN.

For superior results, we purchased unsliced bread from the bakery for this recipe and sliced it ourselves. We gave the recipe our highest rating.

 6   oz. cream cheese, softened
 ¼   cup granulated sugar
 ½   tsp. ground cinnamon
 8   (1½-inch) slices challah or French bread
 1   (12-oz.) package frozen baked apples with cinnamon (we tested with Stouffer's Harvest Apples)
 1   Tbsp. butter, melted
 1   Tbsp. vegetable oil
1½   Tbsp. granulated sugar
 ½   tsp. ground cinnamon
 5   large eggs
 ¾   cup half-and-half
 ¼   cup packed light brown sugar
 1   tsp. vanilla extract
Caramel Syrup (see Caramel-Mocha Syrup variation on facing page)

1. Preheat oven to 400°. Beat first 3 ingredients at medium speed with an electric mixer until smooth.
2. Cut a pocket through top crust of each bread slice, to but not through bottom crust, to form a pocket. Stuff each pocket with about 2 Tbsp. each, cream cheese mixture and apple chunks.
3. Stir together butter and oil. Stir together 1½ Tbsp. granulated sugar and cinnamon until blended.
4. Whisk together eggs and next 3 ingredients in a shallow dish until well blended. Dip stuffed bread slices in egg mixture 5 seconds on each side. Bake on a hot griddle brushed with oil mixture over medium heat 2 minutes on each side or until golden. Transfer to a baking sheet.
5. Bake at 400° for 6 minutes or until thoroughly heated. Sprinkle with cinnamon-sugar mixture. Serve with Caramel Syrup.

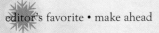

Overnight Yeast Waffles With Caramel-Mocha Syrup and Cinnamon Butter

MAKES 6 SERVINGS
HANDS-ON TIME: 38 MIN.; TOTAL TIME: 8 HR., 38 MIN.

Baking these rich waffles in a Belgian waffle iron creates deep pockets to hold the luscious syrup and spiced butter.

- 1 (¼-oz.) envelope active dry yeast
- ½ cup warm water (100° to 110)
- 2 cups warm milk (100° to 110°)
- ½ cup butter, melted
- 1 tsp. sugar
- ½ tsp. salt
- 2 cups all-purpose flour
- 2 large eggs
- ¼ tsp. baking soda
  Caramel-Mocha Syrup
  Cinnamon Butter

1. Combine yeast and warm water (100° to 110°) in a 1-cup glass measuring cup; let stand 5 minutes. Combine yeast mixture, milk, and next 3 ingredients in a large bowl. Add flour, stirring until smooth. Cover and chill 8 hours.

2. Whisk eggs and baking soda into batter. Cook in a preheated, oiled waffle iron until crisp. Serve waffles with Caramel-Mocha Syrup and Cinnamon Butter.

Caramel-Mocha Syrup

MAKES 1⅔ CUPS
HANDS-ON TIME: 21 MIN.; TOTAL TIME: 21 MIN.

- 1 (14-oz.) package caramels
- ½ cup evaporated milk
- 1¼ tsp. instant espresso
- ¼ cup maple syrup

1. Place caramels in a medium saucepan. Stir together evaporated milk and espresso; add to pan. Cook, stirring constantly, over medium heat until caramels melt and mixture is smooth. Stir in maple syrup. Serve warm.

Caramel Syrup: Prepare recipe as directed, omitting espresso.

Cinnamon Butter

MAKES ½ CUP

HANDS-ON TIME: 3 MIN.; TOTAL TIME: 3 MIN.

- ½ cup butter, softened
- 1 Tbsp. cinnamon sugar

1. Stir together butter and cinnamon sugar until smooth.

editor's favorite

Brown Sugar-Cinnamon Coffee Cake With Spiced Streusel Topping

MAKES 9 SERVINGS
HANDS-ON TIME: 10 MIN.; TOTAL TIME: 1 HR., 4 MIN.

Serve this breakfast favorite warm with mugs of hot coffee.

½ cup butter, softened
1 cup firmly packed light brown sugar
2 large eggs
1 cup sour cream
1 tsp. vanilla extract
1¾ cups all-purpose flour
1 Tbsp. baking powder
1 tsp. ground cinnamon
½ tsp. salt
½ tsp. baking soda
¼ tsp. ground mace
1 cup finely chopped pecans, toasted
Spiced Streusel

1. Preheat oven to 350°. Beat butter and sugar at medium speed with an electric mixer until fluffy. Add eggs, 1 at a time, beating until blended after each addition. Beat in sour cream and vanilla.

2. Whisk together flour, baking powder, and next 4 ingredients. Add to butter mixture; beat at low speed until blended. Stir in pecans. Spread batter into a greased 9-inch square pan. Sprinkle with Spiced Streusel.

3. Bake at 350° for 50 minutes or until a wooden pick inserted in center comes out clean. Cool in pan on a wire rack.

Spiced Streusel

MAKES ABOUT 3 CUPS
HANDS-ON TIME: 4 MIN.; TOTAL TIME: 4 MIN.

1 cup all-purpose flour
1 cup firmly packed light brown sugar
1 tsp. ground cinnamon
¼ tsp. ground mace
½ cup butter, cut into cubes
1 cup coarsely chopped pecans

1. Whisk together flour, brown sugar, and next 2 ingredients in a medium bowl; cut in butter with a pastry blender until crumbly. Stir in pecans.

editor's favorite

Sugar-Crusted Pumpkin Bread

MAKES 1 LOAF
HANDS-ON TIME: 12 MIN.; TOTAL TIME: 1 HR., 22 MIN.

Studded with dried cranberries and walnuts, this tender, flavorful bread with its crunchy top is cholesterol-free and boasts healthful fiber, antioxidants, and omega-3s.

2¼ cups all-purpose flour
½ cup whole wheat flour
1 Tbsp. ground flax seed
1 Tbsp. toasted wheat germ
1 Tbsp. baking powder
1 tsp. baking soda
1 tsp. ground cinnamon
¾ tsp. ground cloves
½ tsp. salt
1 cup granulated sugar
2 large egg whites
1 cup canned pumpkin
¼ cup canola oil
1¼ cups light vanilla soy milk
⅓ cup chopped sweetened dried cranberries
⅓ cup chopped walnuts
Butter-flavored cooking spray
2 Tbsp. turbinado sugar

1. Preheat oven to 350°. Combine first 10 ingredients in a large bowl. Whisk egg whites until frothy in a separate bowl; whisk in pumpkin, oil, and soy milk. Add pumpkin mixture to flour mixture, stirring just until dry ingredients are moistened. Fold in cranberries and walnuts.

2. Pour batter into a 9- x 5-inch loaf pan coated with cooking spray; sprinkle with turbinado sugar. Bake at 350° for 1 hour and 10 minutes or until a wooden pick inserted in center comes out clean. Cool in pan 10 minutes. Remove from pan. Cool completely on a wire rack.

Colossal Apple-Walnut-Browned Butter Muffins

MAKES 10 MUFFINS
HANDS-ON TIME: 24 MIN.; TOTAL TIME: 1 HR., 2 MIN.

Apple and cinnamon, the wonderful aromas of the season, will fill your kitchen on Christmas morning as a batch of these rich, tender muffins bakes, but you can re-create the experience any day of the year.

Colossal Apple-Walnut-Browned Butter Muffins

10   Texas-size paper baking cups
 1   cup butter
 3   cups all-purpose flour
 2   tsp. baking powder
 ½   tsp. salt
 ¼   tsp. ground cinnamon
1¼   cups packed light brown sugar
 3   large eggs
 ¾   cup sour cream
 ¼   cup milk
 2   tsp. vanilla extract
2½   cups chopped peeled Gala or Fuji apple
1½   cup chopped walnuts, toasted
10   thin unpeeled Gala or Fuji apple slices

1. Preheat oven to 375°. Place paper baking cups in 2 (6-cup) Texas-size muffin pans.

2. Melt butter in a large skillet over medium-low heat. Cook 5 minutes or until butter just begins to brown and develop a nutty aroma. (Watch carefully so as not to burn.) Remove from heat; let cool.

3. Combine flour and next 4 ingredients in a large bowl; make a well in center of mixture. Stir together eggs, sour cream, milk, and vanilla; add to dry mixture, stirring just until moistened. Fold in chopped apple and walnuts. Spoon into prepared muffin pans, filling almost full. Insert an apple slice at a 45° angle into each portion of batter to a depth of half the apple slice.

3. Bake at 375° for 32 minutes or until muffins spring back when lightly touched. Cool in pans on wire racks 5 minutes. Remove muffins from pans to wire racks; cool slightly. Serve warm.

Hot Curried Fruit Bake

MAKES 8 TO 10 SERVINGS
HANDS-ON TIME: 13 MIN.; TOTAL TIME: 1 HR., 8 MIN.

Just a hint of curry, almost unidentifiable in this recipe, adds a delightful, unique flavor to this warm fruit. Serve it alongside a savory breakfast casserole or with ham and biscuits.

 1   (20-oz.) can pineapple chunks in juice, undrained
 1   (15-oz.) can sliced peaches in extra-light syrup, drained
 1   (15-oz.) can apricot halves in extra-light syrup, drained
 1   (15¼-oz.) can pear halves in heavy syrup, drained and halved
 2   small Granny Smith apples, peeled and coarsely chopped
 ½   cup drained maraschino cherries
 2   tsp. lemon juice
 ½   cup packed light brown sugar
 1   Tbsp. cornstarch
 ½   tsp. curry powder
 ⅛   tsp. ground cinnamon
 2   Tbsp. butter, cut into pieces

1. Preheat oven to 350°. Drain pineapple; reserving juice. Combine pineapple and next 5 ingredients in a lightly greased 11- x 7-inch baking dish.

2. Whisk together reserved pineapple juice, lemon juice, and next 4 ingredients until smooth. Pour juice mixture over fruit; dot with butter.

3. Bake, uncovered, at 350° for 55 minutes or until bubbly and juices are slightly thickened.

superfast APPETIZERS

These delicious recipes will help you get your holiday gathering started in 30 minutes or less.

quick & easy

Minty Green Pea and Butter Bean Hummus

MAKES 3 CUPS
HANDS-ON TIME: 7 MIN.; TOTAL TIME: 7 MIN.

This festive green hummus made from lima beans, also known as butter beans, has a lighter flavor and texture than traditional hummus, which uses chickpeas. You can also serve it with fresh vegetables.

     2 cups frozen petite peas, thawed
     2 cups frozen baby lima beans, thawed
     3 Tbsp. extra virgin olive oil
     1 Tbsp. fresh lemon juice
     2 large garlic cloves
    ½ cup fresh mint leaves
    ½ cup crumbled feta cheese
    ½ tsp. salt
    ¼ tsp. freshly ground black pepper
        Pita chips

1. Place all ingredients, except pita chips, in a food processor or blender; pulse until smooth. Cover and store in refrigerator. Serve with pita chips.

Minty Green Pea and Butter Bean Hummus

BBQ Pork Sliders With Blue
Cheese Slaw, page 135

Asian-Style Mini Crab Cakes
With Wasabi Aioli

Double Cheese Tartlets

Fried Ravioli With
Marinara Sauce

CITRUS
selections

Oranges, tangerines, limes, and grapefruits—the sweet fruits of the season—are highlighted in these recipes.

quick & easy

Tangerine-Ginger Martinis

MAKES 4 SERVINGS
HANDS-ON TIME: 5 MIN.; TOTAL TIME: 20 MIN.

We've reduced the amount of alcohol slightly in this martini to enhance the tangerine and ginger flavors.

1   tangerine
1   (3-inch) piece fresh ginger, peeled and chopped (½ cup)
½   cup sugar
    Ice cubes
1   cup gin
1   cup fresh tangerine juice

1. Carefully peel tangerine with a vegetable peeler, avoiding the bitter white pith; chop peel. Combine tangerine peel, ginger, sugar, and 1 cup water in a medium saucepan. Bring to a boil over medium-high heat; cover, reduce heat, and simmer 15 minutes. Remove from heat. Pour mixture through a wire-mesh strainer into a 2-cup glass measuring cup or small pitcher; cool completely.
2. Fill a martini shaker half full of ice. Add tangerine-ginger syrup, gin, and tangerine juice. Cover with lid, and shake until thoroughly chilled. Remove lid, and strain into 4 chilled martini glasses. Serve immediately.

1. Stir together first 3 ingredients; add shrimp, stirring gently to coat. Cover and chill 30 minutes.

2. Pour oil to depth of 2 inches into a large Dutch oven; heat over medium-high heat to 350°.

3. Meanwhile, whisk egg whites in a bowl until foamy. Place cornstarch in a shallow dish; place coconut in a separate shallow dish. Remove shrimp from marinade, shaking off excess; dredge in cornstarch. Dip in egg whites, shaking off excess, and dredge in coconut.

4. Fry shrimp, in batches, 3 to 4 minutes or until golden brown, turning once. Drain on a wire rack over paper towels. Sprinkle shrimp with salt, and serve with Sweet Lime–Mustard Sauce.

 quick & easy

Sweet Lime-Mustard Sauce

MAKES 1 CUP
HANDS-ON TIME: 5 MIN.; TOTAL TIME: 5 MIN.

½ cup pineapple preserves
½ cup mustard-mayonnaise blend (we tested with Dijonnaise)
1 tsp. lime zest
1 Tbsp. fresh lime juice
1 Tbsp. fresh chopped cilantro

1. Stir together all ingredients in a small bowl.

 *editor's favorite*

Coconut-Lime Shrimp With Sweet Lime-Mustard Sauce

MAKES 4 SERVINGS
HANDS-ON TIME: 38 MIN.; TOTAL TIME: 1 HR., 8 MIN.

Enjoy a tropical Christmas with these sweet, crunchy morsels.

1 (13.5-oz.) can coconut milk
1 tsp. lime zest
¼ cup fresh lime juice (about 2 limes)
24 large peeled raw shrimp with tails
  Peanut oil
3 egg whites
¾ cup cornstarch
2½ cups sweetened flaked coconut
  Salt to taste
  Sweet Lime-Mustard Sauce

editor's favorite

Citrus-Glazed Orange Rolls

MAKES 1 DOZEN
HANDS-ON TIME: 26 MIN.; TOTAL TIME: 2 HR., 6 MIN.

Dough

⅓ cup butter

¼ cup sugar

2 Tbsp. frozen orange juice concentrate, thawed

2 tsp. orange zest

1 (8-oz.) container sour cream

1 (¼-oz.) envelope active dry yeast

¼ cup warm water (100° to 110°)

3½ to 4 cups all-purpose flour, divided

2 large eggs, lightly beaten

1 tsp. salt

⅓ cup finely chopped walnuts (optional)

Orange Filling

⅓ cup sugar

¼ cup butter, softened

2 tsp. orange zest

Orange Glaze

3 Tbsp. butter, softened

2 cups powdered sugar

2 tsp. orange zest

1 Tbsp. frozen orange juice concentrate, thawed

1 tsp. vanilla extract

2 to 3 Tbsp. half-and-half

1. Prepare dough: Combine first 5 ingredients in a small saucepan; cook over medium heat until butter melts. Remove from heat and cool to 110°.

2. Meanwhile, combine yeast and warm water (100° to 110°) in a 1-cup glass measuring cup; let stand 5 minutes.

3. Combine yeast mixture, 2 cups flour, sour cream mixture, eggs, and salt in a large mixing bowl; beat at medium speed with an electric mixer until well blended. Gradually add in enough flour to make a soft dough.

4. Turn dough out onto a well-floured surface, and knead until smooth and elastic (about 6 minutes). Place in a well-greased bowl, turning to grease top.

5. Cover dough with plastic wrap, and let rise in a warm place (85°), free from drafts, 1 hour or until doubled in bulk.

6. Meanwhile, prepare Orange Filling: Stir together all ingredients until smooth.

7. Punch dough down; let stand 10 minutes. Turn dough out onto a well-floured surface. Roll dough to a 16- x 10-inch rectangle. Spread Orange Filling over dough to within ¾ inch of edges. Sprinkle with walnuts, if desired. Roll up dough jelly-roll fashion, starting at 1 long side. Pinch seam to seal. Cut into 12 equal slices. Place slices, cut side down, in a greased 13- x 9-inch pan.

8. Cover and let rise in a warm place (85°), free from drafts, 30 minutes or until doubled in bulk.

9. Preheat oven to 350°. Bake rolls at 350° for 25 minutes or until golden. Remove from oven, and cool slightly in pan on a wire rack.

10. Meanwhile prepare Orange Glaze: Beat all ingredients, except half-and-half, at medium speed with an electric mixer until crumbly. Gradually stir in half-and-half until smooth and thick, but pourable.

11. Drizzle rolls with Orange Glaze. Serve warm.

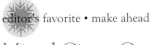 editor's favorite • make ahead

Mixed Citrus Compote

MAKES 8 SERVINGS
HANDS-ON TIME: 39 MIN.; TOTAL TIME: 1 HR., 24 MIN.

- 3 red grapefruits
- 4 blood oranges
- 3 navel oranges
- 1 cup sugar
- 3 Tbsp. honey
- ¼ cup fresh mint leaves
- ½ cup pomegranate seeds*
- Garnish: fresh mint sprigs

1. Using a sharp, thin-bladed knife, cut a ¼-inch-thick slice from each end of grapefruits and oranges. Place flat-end down on a cutting board, and remove peel in strips, cutting from top to bottom following the curvature of fruit. Remove any remaining bitter white pith.

2. Holding peeled fruit in the palm of your hand over a bowl, slice between membranes, and gently remove whole segments, catching juice in bowl. Pour juice into a glass measuring cup, adding water if necessary, to measure ¾ cup; reserve fruit in bowl.

3. Combine juice, sugar, and next 2 ingredients in a medium saucepan; bring to a boil over medium heat. Boil 5 minutes, stirring occasionally. Remove from heat, and let cool, uncovered, 45 minutes. Remove and discard mint.

4. Pour syrup over fruit; gently stir in pomegranate seeds. Cover and chill until ready to serve. Garnish, if desired.

* Look for packages of fresh pomegranate seeds in the produce section of your supermarket.

editor's favorite • make ahead

Ambrosia Cake

MAKES 16 SERVINGS
HANDS-ON TIME: 57 MIN.; TOTAL TIME: 4 HR., 3 MIN.

This stately cake boasts oranges, pineapple, and coconut—the characteristic combination found in classic holiday ambrosia.

Cake

Wax paper
¾ cup butter, softened
¾ cup shortening
1¾ cups sugar
3½ cups cake flour
1 Tbsp. baking powder
½ tsp. salt
1 cup milk
1 tsp. vanilla extract
6 egg whites
½ tsp. cream of tartar
2 cups sweetened flaked coconut

Orange-Pineapple Filling

2 (8-oz.) cans crushed pineapple in juice, drained
1¼ cups sugar
3 Tbsp. cornstarch
⅛ tsp. salt
1 Tbsp. orange zest
1 cup orange juice
4 egg yolks, lightly beaten
2 Tbsp. butter

Seven-Minute White Icing

1½ cups sugar
⅓ cup cold water
3 egg whites
1 Tbsp. light corn syrup
¼ tsp. cream of tartar
⅛ tsp. salt
½ tsp. lemon extract

Garnish

Kumquats

1. Prepare cake: Preheat oven to 350°. Grease 2 (9-inch) round cake pans with shortening; line pans with wax paper, and grease paper. Dust with flour, shaking out excess.

2. Beat butter and shortening at medium speed with an electric mixer until creamy; gradually add sugar, beating well.

3. Combine flour, baking powder, and salt; add to creamed mixture alternately with milk, beginning and ending with flour mixture. Beat at low speed until blended after each addition. Stir in vanilla.

4. Beat egg whites and cream of tartar at high speed with an electric mixer until stiff peaks form; fold about one-fourth of egg whites into batter. Gradually fold in remaining egg whites. Pour cake batter into prepared pans.

5. Bake at 350° for 30 minutes or until a wooden pick inserted in center comes out clean. Cool in pans on wire racks 10 minutes; remove from pans to wire racks, and cool completely (about 1 hour).

6. Cake layers can be wrapped and chilled 1 to 24 hours.

7. Prepare Orange-Pineapple Filling: Pat pineapple dry with paper towels. Whisk together sugar and next 3 ingredients in a medium saucepan; gradually whisk in orange juice. Bring to a boil over medium heat, whisking constantly. Boil, whisking constantly, 1 to 1½ minutes or until thickened. Gradually whisk about one-fourth of hot mixture into egg yolks; add to remaining hot mixture, whisking constantly. Cook over low heat, whisking constantly, 3 minutes or until thickened. Remove pan from heat; stir in butter and pineapple. Cool completely (about 1 hour).

8. Prepare Seven-Minute White Icing: Combine first 6 ingredients in top of a double boiler. Beat at low speed with a handheld electric mixer just until blended. Place over boiling water; beat at high speed 6 to 7 minutes or until stiff peaks form. Remove from heat; add extract. Beat 2 minutes or until spreading consistency.

9. Spread Orange-Pineapple Filling between cake layers. Spread Seven-Minute White Icing on top and sides of cake. Sprinkle coconut over icing. Garnish, if desired. Store cake at room temperature.

make ahead:

Assemble cake layers and filling. Cover and store in refrigerator up to 2 days. Frost cake the day of serving.

Christmas COMFORT FOOD

You'll find something here to please everyone in the family with this collection of homey favorites.

editor's *favorite*

Baked Mostaccioli

MAKES 8 SERVINGS
HANDS-ON TIME: 38 MIN.; TOTAL TIME: 1 HR., 28 MIN.

This hearty, meaty pasta is sure to satisfy your crowd's cravings for something rich, cheesy, and Italian. It received our Test Kitchen's highest rating.

12	oz. uncooked mostaccioli pasta
4	oz. cream cheese, softened
1	(15-oz.) container ricotta cheese
1	cup freshly grated Parmesan cheese
1	large egg
2	green onions, minced
½	tsp. garlic powder
¼	tsp. salt
¼	tsp. pepper
1	lb. ground round
½	lb. Italian sausage
1	(24-oz.) jar fire-roasted tomato pasta sauce with cabernet (we tested with Bertolli)
1	(14.5-oz.) can fire-roasted diced tomatoes with garlic, drained
2	(8-oz.) packages shredded mozzarella cheese

1. Preheat oven to 350°. Cook pasta in boiling salted water according to package directions; drain.

2. Meanwhile, mash cream cheese with a fork until smooth; stir in ricotta cheese and next 6 ingredients until blended.

3. Cook ground round and sausage in a large skillet over medium-high heat until meat crumbles and is no longer pink; drain and return to pan. Stir in pasta sauce and tomatoes; bring to a boil. Remove from heat.

4. Spread half of meat mixture on bottom of a lightly greased 13- x 9-inch baking dish. Layer half of pasta over meat; layer ricotta mixture over pasta. Sprinkle 1 package of cheese over ricotta mixture. Repeat layers using remaining half of meat mixture, pasta, and cheese.

5. Bake at 350° for 45 to 50 minutes or until bubbly.

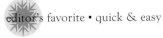

editor's favorite • quick & easy

Caramel Apple Cider

MAKES 4½ CUPS
HANDS-ON TIME: 13 MIN.; TOTAL TIME: 13 MIN.

This kid-friendly cup of warmth tastes like liquid apple pie.
Include it in the Tree-Cutting Party menu (page 23),
if you like.

⅓ cup firmly packed light brown sugar
⅓ cup heavy whipping cream
1 tsp. vanilla extract
4 cups apple cider
Garnishes: whipped cream, caramel sauce, ground
cinnamon

1. Stir together brown sugar and whipping cream in a large saucepan. Cook, stirring constantly, over medium heat 2 minutes or until bubbly. Stir in vanilla and apple cider. Cook 10 minutes or until thoroughly heated, stirring often. Garnish, if desired.

This is a soul-satisfying treat on a chilly day.

editor's favorite

Pimiento Mac 'n' Cheese

MAKES 8 TO 10 SERVINGS
HANDS-ON TIME: 11 MIN.; TOTAL TIME: 51 MIN.

Two of our Southern comfort foods marry to create the ultimate mac and cheese. If you have a box grater, use the medium-size side to grate both the onion and the cheeses.

- 2 cups uncooked elbow macaroni
- 2½ cups milk
- ½ cup mayonnaise
- ¼ cup butter, melted
- 2 Tbsp. grated onion
- 1 Tbsp. Worcestershire sauce
- ½ tsp. salt
- ¼ tsp. ground red pepper
- 1 large egg, lightly beaten
- 1 (4-oz.) jar diced pimientos, drained
- 1 (2-oz.) jar diced pimientos, drained
- 1 (8-oz.) package sharp Cheddar cheese, shredded
- 1 (8-oz.) package extra-sharp Cheddar cheese, shredded

1. Preheat oven to 350°. Cook macaroni in boiling salted water according to package directions; drain.
2. Meanwhile, stir together milk and next 9 ingredients in a medium bowl. Spoon half of cooked macaroni into a greased 13- x 9-inch baking dish. Pour half of milk mixture over macaroni in dish; top with half of cheeses. Top with remaining half of macaroni, milk mixture, and cheeses.
3. Bake, uncovered, at 350° for 40 minutes or until pasta mixture is set and cheese is golden.

Chicken Divan

MAKES 8 SERVINGS
HANDS-ON TIME: 20 MIN.; TOTAL TIME: 1 HR.

Using a whole chicken is more economical than chicken breasts alone, and the dark meat adds lots of flavor.

- 1 (4 lb.) whole chicken
- 2 celery ribs with leaves, halved crosswise
- 1 tsp. salt
- ½ tsp. pepper
- 2 broccoli crowns, cut into spears
- 3 Tbsp. butter
- 3 Tbsp. all-purpose flour
- 3 cups milk
- 1½ cups (6 oz.) shredded white Cheddar cheese
- 1½ tsp. fresh lemon juice
- ¾ tsp. salt
- ¾ tsp. curry powder
- ¼ tsp. ground red pepper
- 2½ cups cooked rice
- 1 cup (4 oz.) shredded Parmesan cheese
- Paprika

1. Combine first 4 ingredients and water to cover (we used 12 cups) in a large Dutch oven. Bring to a boil over medium-high heat; reduce heat, and simmer 1 hour or until tender. Remove chicken, and cool 25 minutes or until cool enough to handle.
2. Pour broth through a wire-mesh strainer into a large bowl, discarding solids. Return broth to pan; bring to a boil. Add broccoli, and cook until crisp-tender. Drain, reserving broth for another use.
3. Skin, bone, and coarsely chop chicken; cover and keep warm.
4. Preheat oven to 350°. Melt butter in a medium saucepan over medium-low heat; add flour, stirring until smooth. Cook 1 minute, stirring constantly. Gradually add milk; cook over medium heat, stirring constantly, until thickened and bubbly. Add Cheddar cheese and next 4 ingredients, stirring until smooth.
5. Spread rice on bottom of a lightly greased 13- x 9-inch baking dish. Layer broccoli and chicken over rice. Pour cheese sauce over chicken mixture. Sprinkle with Parmesan cheese and paprika. Bake, uncovered, at 350° for 45 minutes or until bubbly and lightly browned.

fix it faster:

Substitute 4 cups chopped cooked chicken from a rotisserie chicken. Cook broccoli in boiling salted water to cover instead of the broth.

editor's favorite

Squash and Cornbread Dressing

MAKES 12 SERVINGS
HANDS-ON TIME: 1 HR.; TOTAL TIME: 1 HR., 45 MIN.

- 5 Tbsp. canola oil, divided
- 2 cups self-rising white cornmeal mix (we tested with White Lily)
- 1 large egg
- 1⅓ cups milk
- 2 (16-oz.) packages frozen sliced yellow squash
- 2 cups chopped celery
- ½ cup butter
- 3 large onions, chopped (about 6 cups)
- 1½ sleeves saltine crackers, coarsely crushed
- 1½ cups (6 oz.) shredded sharp Cheddar cheese
- 2 large eggs
- 1½ tsp. poultry seasoning
- 1½ tsp. pepper
- ¼ tsp. salt
- 1 cup chicken broth

1. Preheat oven to 450°. Place 1 Tbsp. oil in a 9-inch cast-iron skillet; place skillet in oven while it preheats. Place cornmeal mix in a large bowl; make a well in center. Whisk together 1 egg, milk, and remaining ¼ cup oil; add to cornmeal mix, stirring just until moistened. Pour batter into preheated skillet.

2. Bake at 450° for 20 to 25 minutes or until golden brown. Place cornbread in a large bowl. Set aside. Reduce oven temperature to 350°.

3. Meanwhile, place squash, celery, and ¼ cup water in a large microwave-safe bowl. Cover, vent, and microwave at HIGH 25 minutes or until vegetables are tender, stirring every 10 minutes. (Do not drain.)

4. Meanwhile, melt butter in a large skillet over medium-high heat; add onion, and cook, stirring often, 10 minutes or until tender. Stir in crackers. Reserve 3 cups of cracker mixture. Crumble cornbread in bowl; add remaining cracker mixture and 1½ cups cheese, tossing well. Stir squash mixture into cornbread mixture.

5. Whisk together 2 eggs and next 3 ingredients in a medium bowl; stir in broth. Stir egg mixture into cornbread mixture. Spoon into 2 greased 11- x 7-inch baking dishes. Top each casserole with 1½ cups reserved cracker mixture.

6. Bake, uncovered, at 350° for 45 to 50 minutes or until golden.

Two Southern favorites, squash casserole and cornbread dressing, come together in this homey companion to roast turkey.

Broccoli-Cauliflower Salad With Dried Cranberries and Pistachios

MAKES 6 TO 8 SERVINGS
HANDS-ON TIME: 20 MIN.; TOTAL TIME: 20 MIN.

Dried cranberries and pistachios replace raisins and pecans in this traditional salad.

- 6   bacon slices
- 1   cup mayonnaise
- ¼   cup sugar
- 2   Tbsp. red wine vinegar
- ½   tsp. salt
- ¼   tsp. pepper
- 3   cups coarsely chopped broccoli florets
- 2   cups coarsely chopped cauliflower (about ½ head)
- 1   cup sweetened dried cranberries (we tested with Craisins)
- ½   cup chopped pistachios
- 3   Tbsp. chopped red onion

1. Cook bacon in a large skillet over medium-high heat 6 to 7 minutes or until crisp; remove bacon, and drain on paper towels. Crumble bacon.

2. Meanwhile, combine mayonnaise and next 4 ingredients in a large bowl, stirring until blended. Add bacon, broccoli, and remaining ingredients. Toss until vegetables are coated.

Note: Chop the broccoli and cauliflower just enough to create uniform pieces, keeping smaller florets intact.

editor's favorite

Turkey and Wild Rice Soup

MAKES 10 CUPS
HANDS-ON TIME: 9 MIN.; TOTAL TIME: 1 HR., 10 MIN.

Chewy wild rice adds a satisfying texture to this creamy rich soup. It's a great way to transform leftover holiday turkey into an upscale lunch or supper.

2 Tbsp. butter
1 tsp. salt, divided
1 cup uncooked wild rice
4 bacon slices
1 medium onion, chopped (2 cups)
3 celery ribs, chopped (1½ cups)
2 large garlic cloves, minced
6 cups chicken broth
¼ tsp. freshly ground pepper
3 cups chopped cooked turkey
1 cup heavy cream
2 Tbsp. chopped fresh parsley

1. Bring 4 cups water, butter, and ½ tsp. salt to a boil in a large saucepan. Stir in rice. Return to a boil; reduce heat, cover, and cook 55 minutes or until rice is tender. Drain, if necessary, and set aside.

2. Meanwhile, cook bacon in a large Dutch oven over medium-high heat 6 to 7 minutes or until crisp; remove bacon, and drain on paper towels, reserving drippings in skillet. Crumble bacon.

3. Sauté onion, celery, and garlic in hot drippings until tender. Stir in remaining ½ tsp. salt, broth and next 2 ingredients. Bring to a boil; cover, reduce heat, and simmer 5 minutes or until thoroughly heated. Stir in rice, bacon, and cream. Cook over medium heat 15 minutes or until slightly thickened. Stir in parsley.

 editor's favorite

Loaded Potato Soup

MAKES 15 CUPS
HANDS-ON TIME: 35 MIN.; TOTAL TIME: 40 MIN.

We gave our highest rating to this soup, which includes all your favorite baked potato toppings.

1 (12-oz.) package bacon slices (approximately 12 slices)
1 medium onion, chopped (1½ cups)
6 cups chicken broth
2 lb. baking potatoes, peeled and cubed
⅔ cup butter
¾ cup all-purpose flour
4 cups milk, divided
1 tsp. freshly ground pepper
1 tsp. salt
1 cup diced cooked ham
1¼ cups sour cream, divided
2½ cups shredded sharp Cheddar cheese, divided
¾ cup sliced green onions, divided

1. Cook bacon in a large skillet over medium heat 6 to 7 minutes or until crisp; remove bacon, and drain on paper towels, reserving 2 Tbsp. drippings in skillet. Crumble bacon, and set aside.

2. Sauté onion in drippings over medium-high heat 6 minutes or until almost tender.

3. Combine onion, chicken broth, and potato in a large Dutch oven. Bring to a boil; reduce heat, and cook 10 minutes or until potato is very tender.

4. Meanwhile, melt butter in skillet over low heat; add flour, whisking until smooth. Cook, whisking constantly, 1 minute. Gradually whisk in 2 cups milk; pour milk mixture into potato mixture. Add remaining 2 cups milk, pepper, and salt; cook over medium heat, whisking constantly, until mixture is thickened and bubbly.

5. Stir in half of bacon, 1 cup diced ham, 1 cup sour cream, 2 cups cheese, and ½ cup green onions. Cook until thoroughly heated and cheese melts. Ladle soup into bowls, and top with remaining bacon, sour cream, cheese, and green onions.

editor's favorite

Vegetable Minestrone

MAKES ABOUT 12 CUPS
HANDS-ON TIME: 32 MIN.; TOTAL TIME: 1 HR., 20 MIN.

When reheating, add a little broth or water to soup to thin it, if necessary.

3   large carrots, chopped
3   celery ribs, chopped
3   garlic cloves, minced
2   medium zucchini, coarsely chopped
1   medium onion, chopped
1   (12-oz.) package trimmed green beans, cut into 1-inch pieces
3   Tbsp. olive oil
1   (28-oz.) can diced tomatoes with basil, garlic, and oregano, undrained
1   (14.5-oz.) can fire-roasted diced tomatoes with garlic, undrained
2   (32-oz.) containers beef broth
1   (15.8-oz.) can great Northern beans, drained
1   (16-oz.) can dark red kidney beans, drained
½   tsp. salt
¼   tsp. dried crushed red pepper
1½ cups uncooked ditalini pasta
1   (6-oz.) package baby spinach
2½ Tbsp. jarred pesto
    Freshly grated Parmesan cheese

1. Sauté first 6 ingredients in hot oil in a large Dutch oven over medium-high heat 7 minutes or until crisp-tender. Add both cans tomatoes and next 5 ingredients. Bring to a boil; reduce heat, and simmer, uncovered, 20 minutes or until vegetables are tender.

2. Add pasta to soup. Cook 10 minutes or until pasta is tender. Stir in spinach; cook 1 minute or until spinach wilts. Stir in pesto. Ladle into bowls; sprinkle with Parmesan cheese.

Pecan Caramel-Rum Tart

 editor's favorite • great gift

Chocolate Cookies With Peanut Butter Filling

MAKES 19 SANDWICHES
HANDS-ON TIME: 40 MIN.; TOTAL TIME: 1 HR., 2 MIN.

The classic combination of chocolate and peanut butter makes up these crunchy sandwiches with creamy centers.

Cookies

2 cups semisweet chocolate morsels
1 cup sugar
¾ cup butter, softened
2 large eggs
1 tsp. vanilla extract
2 cups all-purpose flour
⅓ cup unsweetened cocoa
1 tsp. baking soda
½ tsp. salt
½ tsp. instant coffee granules

Peanut Butter Filling

1 (3-oz.) package cream cheese, softened
5 Tbsp. butter, softened
2 cups powdered sugar
½ cup creamy peanut butter
Dash of salt

editor's favorite

Pecan Caramel-Rum Tart

MAKES 6 TO 8 SERVINGS
HANDS-ON TIME: 20 MIN.; TOTAL TIME: 28 MIN.

Pecans coated with caramel take center stage in this rich, nutty tart.

1½ cups sugar
½ (15-oz.) package refrigerated piecrusts
Parchment paper
¼ cup butter
⅔ cup whipping cream
Dash of salt
1½ Tbsp. dark rum (optional)
3 cups chopped pecans

1. Preheat oven to 425°. Combine sugar and ½ cup water in a large skillet; cook over medium heat until sugar caramelizes, tipping pan to incorporate mixture. Cook 15 minutes or until golden, stirring occasionally to blend color.

2. Meanwhile, fit piecrust into a 9-inch tart pan with removable bottom. Trim off excess pastry, and press pastry against sides of pan. Place tart pan on a large baking sheet lined with parchment paper.

3. Add butter to caramel mixture, stirring until melted and blended. Gradually stir in cream and salt; cook, stirring constantly, 2 minutes. Remove from heat, and stir in rum, if desired, and pecans.

4. Pour pecan filling into prepared piecrust. Bake at 425° for 28 minutes or until golden. Transfer to a wire rack to cool completely.

1. Preheat oven to 375°. Place chocolate morsels in a microwave-safe bowl. Microwave at HIGH 1 minute and 30 seconds; stir until smooth. Cool slightly.

2. Beat sugar and butter at medium speed with an electric mixer until creamy Add eggs and vanilla; beat at low speed until blended. Add chocolate; beat until blended.

3. Whisk together flour and next 4 ingredients. Add to chocolate mixture, beating at low speed just until blended. Shape dough into 38 (1½-inch) balls. Place balls 3 inches apart on lightly greased baking sheets; flatten balls slightly.

4. Bake at 375° for 10 to 12 minutes or until set. Cool cookies on baking sheets 10 minutes. Remove to wire racks, and cool completely.

5. Meanwhile, prepare filling: Beat cream cheese and butter at medium speed with an electric mixer until blended. Gradually add powdered sugar, beating until smooth. Add peanut butter and salt, beating at low speed until blended.

6. Spread bottom of each of 19 cookies with a heaping tablespoon of Peanut Butter Filling. Top with remaining cookies; gently press together.

Sweet and Salty Mixed Nut Brittle

editor's favorite • great gift • make ahead

Sweet and Salty Mixed Nut Brittle

MAKES 2 POUNDS
HANDS-ON TIME: 9 MIN.; TOTAL TIME: 24 MIN.

Many are intimidated by making homemade candy, but we've made it easy—it's cooked in the microwave.

- 2 cups sugar
- 1 cup light corn syrup
- 1 (11.5-oz.) can lightly salted mixed nuts
- 2 Tbsp. butter, softened
- 1 Tbsp. baking soda
- 2 tsp. vanilla extract

1. Heavily butter a large baking sheet. Combine sugar and corn syrup in a 4-qt. microwave-safe bowl, stirring well. Cover with plastic wrap, and microwave at HIGH 4 minutes.
2. Carefully uncover, and microwave 8 to 9 minutes or until lightly golden in center. Stir in nuts. Microwave 1 minute or until mixture boils.
3. Remove bowl from microwave. Quickly stir in butter, baking soda, and vanilla. Quickly pour mixture onto prepared pan, spreading to edges of pan with a buttered large metal spoon. Let candy cool on pan. Break into pieces, and store in an airtight container.

Note: We tested this recipe in an 1100-watt microwave oven. If your oven is a different wattage, adjust times accordingly.

tip:

Have the butter, baking soda, and vanilla measured ahead of time, but don't combine them, so you can add them quickly. The candy will become a deep golden color after the baking soda is added.

Microwave cooking updates this old-fashioned favorite.

Sweet and Spicy Glazed Popcorn

MAKES 22 CUPS
HANDS-ON TIME: 11 MIN.; TOTAL TIME: 1 HR., 45 MIN.

Caramel corn gets a spicy kick from ground red pepper in this adult version of the carnival favorite.

- 2 (3.5-oz.) packages natural-flavored microwave popcorn (we tested with Newman's Own)
- 2 cups lightly salted dry-roasted peanuts
- 2 cups firmly packed light brown sugar
- ½ cup unsalted butter
- ½ cup light corn syrup
- ½ tsp. salt
- ½ tsp. baking soda
- ¾ tsp. paprika
- ½ tsp. ground red pepper

1. Preheat oven to 250°. Pop popcorn according to package directions; remove unpopped kernels. Combine popcorn and peanuts in a lightly greased 16- x 12-inch roasting pan.
2. Combine brown sugar, butter, and corn syrup in a 2½-qt. heavy saucepan. Bring to a boil over medium-high heat, stirring until butter melts. Wash down sides of pan with a brush dipped in hot water. Insert a candy thermometer into brown sugar mixture. Cook until thermometer registers 256° (hard ball stage), about 4 minutes (do not stir).
3. Remove from heat; stir in salt and next 3 ingredients. Gradually pour brown sugar mixture over popcorn and nuts, stirring gently to coat well, using a long-handled spoon.
4. Bake at 250° for 1½ hours or until dry, stirring occasionally (approximately every 30 minutes). Cool completely in pan. Break into clusters, and store in an airtight container up to 2 weeks.

Sweet and Spicy Glazed Popcorn

Honey-Glazed Almonds

MAKES 2 CUPS
HANDS-ON TIME: 20 MIN.; TOTAL TIME: 40 MIN.

- 2 cups whole natural almonds
- 2 Tbsp. honey
- 2 tsp. vegetable oil
- ¼ cup sugar
- ½ tsp. salt
- Wax paper

1. Preheat oven to 350°. Place almonds in a single layer on a jelly-roll pan. Bake at 350° for 10 minutes or until toasted and fragrant.
2. Bring 2 Tbsp. water, honey, and oil to a boil in a large nonstick skillet over medium heat. Stir in nuts. Cook, stirring constantly, 3 minutes or until liquid evaporates.
3. Sprinkle sugar and salt over almonds; cook, stirring constantly, 5 minutes or until almonds are reddish brown and coated. Spread nuts on wax paper; cool 10 minutes. Break nuts apart; cool completely. Store in an airtight container.

great gift • make ahead

Peppered Pecans

MAKES 2 CUPS
HANDS-ON TIME: 4 MIN.; TOTAL TIME: 34 MIN.

Pfeffernüesse, traditional German Christmas cookies containing black pepper and coated with powdered sugar, inspired these spicy, sweet nuts.

- 2 Tbsp. butter, melted
- 1 tsp. freshly ground pepper
- ¾ tsp. apple pie spice
- 2 cups pecan halves
- ¼ cup powdered sugar

1. Preheat oven to 300°. Whisk together first 3 ingredients in a large bowl; add pecans, stirring to coat. Spread nut mixture on a foil-lined jelly-roll pan. Bake at 300° for 30 minutes or until toasted, stirring every 10 minutes. Let cool in pan on a wire rack.
2. Return nuts to bowl; sprinkle with powdered sugar, tossing gently to coat.

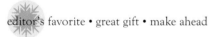

editor's favorite • *great gift* • make ahead

Maple and Brown Sugar-Cinnamon Pecans

MAKES 5 CUPS
HANDS-ON TIME: 5 MIN.; TOTAL TIME: 50 MIN.

If you store your pecans in the freezer, let them come to room temperature before preparing the recipe.

- 1 egg white
- 2 Tbsp. maple syrup
- ½ cup firmly packed light brown sugar
- 1 tsp. ground cinnamon
- 1 lb. pecan halves
- Parchment paper

1. Preheat oven to 300°. Whisk egg white until frothy in a large bowl; whisk in maple syrup, brown sugar, and cinnamon. Add pecans, stirring to coat.
2. Place nuts in a single layer on a parchment paper-lined jelly-roll pan.
3. Bake at 300° for 40 minutes or until pecans are toasted and a crunchy crust forms, stirring every 15 minutes. Cool in pan on a wire rack.

great gift • make ahead

Asian Snack Mix

MAKES 7 CUPS
HANDS-ON TIME: 8 MIN.; TOTAL TIME: 1 HR., 8 MIN.

This sweet, salty, spicy, tangy, and crunchy snack mix covers all the bases for cravings. In addition to making the perfect gift, it's great tucked in a lunch box or desk drawer for that extra treat.

- 2 cups rice cereal squares
- 2 cups sesame sticks
- 1 cup tiny pretzels
- 1 cup wasabi peas
- ¾ cup salted cashews
- ½ cup coarsely chopped dried apricots
- ⅓ cup butter
- 1 Tbsp. sugar
- 1 Tbsp. soy sauce
- 2 tsp. dark sesame oil
- ½ tsp. garlic powder
- ¼ tsp. ground red pepper

1. Preheat oven to 225°. Combine first 6 ingredients in a large bowl.
2. Combine butter and remaining ingredients in a 2-cup glass measuring cup. Cover and microwave at HIGH 1 minute or until butter melts, stirring until sugar dissolves. Drizzle butter mixture over cereal mixture, stirring to coat well. Spread snack mix onto foil-lined jelly-roll pan coated with cooking spray. Bake at 225° for 1 hour, stirring every 15 minutes.
3. Remove from oven. Cool in pan on a wire rack. Store in an airtight container for up to 1 month.

Try this tasty spin on standard cheese straws.

great gift • make ahead

Parmesan-Olive Cheese Straws

MAKES 10½ DOZEN
HANDS-ON TIME: 24 MIN.; TOTAL TIME: 1 HR., 56 MIN.

Serve this twist on traditional cheese straws at your next buffet, or enjoy with a glass of red wine.

½ cup butter, softened
⅔ cup freshly grated Parmigiano-Reggiano cheese
1¾ cups all-purpose flour
3 Tbsp. kalamata olive tapenade, finely chopped
Parchment paper

1. Preheat oven to 375°. Beat butter and cheese at medium speed with a heavy-duty stand mixer until fluffy. Gradually add flour, beating just until combined. Stir in tapenade.
2. Spoon dough into a cookie press fitted with a star-shaped disk, and press dough into 2-inch straws onto parchment paper-lined baking sheets, following manufacturer's instructions. Bake at 375° for 14 minutes. Remove straws to wire racks to cool. Store in airtight containers.

Sun-dried Tomato Marinated Bocconcini in Garlic Oil

MAKES 7 HALF-PINTS
HANDS-ON TIME: 17 MIN.; TOTAL TIME: 24 HR., 17 MIN.

Toss these little "mouthfuls" and their flavorful marinade into green or pasta salads, or serve solo with mini bagel chips.

- 1   (7-oz.) jar sun-dried tomatoes in oil
- 1   cup olive oil
- ¾   cup white wine vinegar
- 1   Tbsp. fresh thyme leaves
- 1   tsp. freshly ground pepper
- ¾   tsp. salt
- 5   garlic cloves, coarsely chopped
- 2   lb. bocconcini mozzarella, drained
- 7   (½-pt.) jars, sterilized

1. Drain tomatoes, reserving oil. Chop tomatoes. Process tomato oil, olive oil, and next 5 ingredients in a blender until smooth. Pour into a bowl; stir in chopped tomatoes. Add cheese, stirring to coat. Fill jars with cheese and marinade. Seal jars, and marinate in refrigerator at least 24 hours before serving. Store in refrigerator up to 1 week.

editor's favorite • great gift • make ahead • quick & easy

Rosemary-Marinated Olives

MAKES 2 PINTS
HANDS-ON TIME: 30 MIN.; TOTAL TIME: 30 MIN.

Take a jar of these tasty morsels to your next dinner party as a hostess gift instead of a bottle of wine.

- 1 lemon
- ½ cup olive oil
- 1½ lb. mixed olives
- 1 tsp. mixed peppercorns
- 2 sprigs fresh rosemary
- 1 large garlic clove, minced

1. Cut 4 (2- x ¼-inch) strips of zest lengthwise from lemon, using a vegetable peeler. Squeeze juice from lemon to measure ¼ cup.
2. Whisk together lemon juice and oil in a medium bowl. Add lemon zest, olives, and remaining 3 ingredients; toss to coat.
3. Spoon olive mixture into 2 sterilized (1-pt.) jars or 4 sterilized (½-pt.) jars. Marinate in refrigerator up to 3 weeks. Let olives come to room temperature, and stir well before serving.

Note: Letting the olives come to room temperature allows the olive oil, which is solid when cold, to liquefy again.

PETITS CAKES

Arrange an assortment of these tiny cakes on a tiered cake stand for a show-stopping presentation at your holiday party, or package in boxes for delightful gifts. We've chosen the following flavor combinations, but the possibilities are endless.

Red Velvet Petits Cakes

MAKES 6 DOZEN
HANDS-ON TIME: 48 MIN.; TOTAL TIME: 1 HR., 23 MIN.

Miniature baking cups*
1 (18.25-oz.) package red velvet cake mix (we tested with Duncan Hines)
2 (16-oz.) containers cream cheese frosting
Finely chopped toasted pecans (optional)

1. Preheat oven to 350°. Line miniature muffin pans with baking cups. Prepare cake mix batter according to package directions. Spoon about 1 heaping Tbsp. batter into each baking cup, filling two-thirds full. Bake at 350° for 11 minutes or until a wooden pick inserted in center comes out clean. Remove from oven; let cool 5 minutes in pans on wire racks. Remove from pans; let cool completely on wire racks.
2. Spread cream cheese frosting on tops of cakes, and sprinkle with pecans, if desired.

Coconut Petits Cakes

MAKES 5½ DOZEN
HANDS-ON TIME: 1 HR., 3 MIN.; TOTAL TIME: 1 HR., 33 MIN.

Miniature baking cups*
1 (18.25-oz.) package coconut supreme cake mix (we tested with Duncan Hines)
1 (7.2-oz.) package fluffy white frosting mix (we tested with Betty Crocker)
1 (10-oz.) jar lemon curd (we tested with Dickinson's)
1 (3.5-oz.) can sweetened flaked coconut

1. Preheat oven to 350°. Line miniature muffin pans with baking cups. Prepare cake mix batter according to package directions. Spoon about 1 heaping Tbsp. batter into each baking cup, filling two-thirds full. Bake at 350° for 10 to 12 minutes or until a wooden pick inserted in center comes out clean. Remove from oven; let cool 5 minutes in pans on wire racks. Remove from pans; let cool completely on wire racks.
2. Meanwhile, prepare frosting mix according to package directions. Spoon about ½ tsp. lemon curd on top of each cake. Spread frosting on tops of cakes, and sprinkle with coconut.

Brownie Ganache Bites

MAKES 35
HANDS-ON TIME: 23 MIN.; TOTAL TIME: 35 MIN.

Miniature baking cups*
1 (20-oz.) package double–chocolate brownie mix (we tested with Ghirardelli)
⅓ cup semisweet chocolate morsels
⅓ cup whipping cream

1. Preheat oven to 350°. Line miniature muffin pans with baking cups. Prepare brownie mix batter according to package directions. Let batter stand 5 minutes until thickened. Spoon 1 level Tbsp. batter into each baking cup. Bake at 350° for 12 minutes. Remove from pans. Cool completely on wire racks.
2. Combine chocolate morsels and cream in a 1-cup glass measuring cup. Microwave at HIGH 1 minute; stir until smooth. Spread ganache over tops of brownies, ending in a decorative swirl.

*We used baking cups that were about 1½ inches in diameter. They are available, both in paper and in foil, in a variety of patterns and colors.

Variation: Brownie bites may be removed from baking cups and turned upside down. Spoon ganache over bites, and top with a walnut half or sprinkle with chopped hazelnuts. Carefully set prepared bites in new slightly larger baking cups (the tops are larger than the bottoms of the cups in which they were baked) for presentation.

Chocolate-Mint Brownie Pops

MAKES 31 POPS
HANDS-ON TIME: 1 HR., 21 MIN.; TOTAL TIME: 3 HR., 23 MIN.

*The Test Kitchen gave these decadent brownies-on-a-stick
our highest rating.*

- ½ cup butter
- 2 (1-oz.) squares unsweetened chocolate
- 1 (10-oz.) package crème de menthe baking morsels
  (we tested with Andes)
- 1 cup sugar
- 2 large eggs, lightly beaten
- 1 tsp. vanilla extract
- ¾ cup all-purpose flour
- ¼ tsp. salt
- Parchment paper
- 2 Tbsp. shortening
- 5 (2-oz.) chocolate candy coating squares
- 31 (4-inch) white craft sticks
- 4 (2-oz.) vanilla candy coating squares
- Crushed peppermint candies

1. Preheat oven to 350°. Combine butter, unsweetened chocolate, and 1 cup baking chips in a medium saucepan. Cook over low heat, stirring constantly until melted. Remove from heat; add sugar, eggs, and vanilla, beating until smooth.
2. Combine flour and salt; stir into chocolate mixture until blended. Stir in remaining baking morsels.
3. Pour batter into a lightly greased 8-inch square pan. Bake at 350° for 32 minutes. Cool completely in pan on a wire rack.
4. Using a 2-Tbsp. scoop, scoop out balls from cooked brownie in pan. Gently reshape into smooth balls; place on a large baking sheet lined with parchment paper. Chill 30 minutes.
5. Place shortening and chocolate candy coating in a 2-cup glass measuring cup. Microwave at HIGH 1 minute or until melted. Stir until smooth. Insert a craft stick into each brownie ball. Dip each ball into melted chocolate mixture, reheating as necessary to keep mixture liquid. Place dipped balls on a large baking sheet lined with parchment paper. Let stand until firm.
6. Place vanilla candy coating in a bowl. Microwave at HIGH 40 seconds or until melted. Spoon into a large zip-top plastic freezer bag; seal bag. Snip a small hole (about ⅛ inch in diameter) in 1 corner of bag . Squeeze white chocolate onto dipped brownie balls to decorate as desired; sprinkle with crushed peppermint.

**Chocolate-Mint
Brownie Pops**

Pistachio-Lime Wedding Cookies

MAKES ABOUT 3 DOZEN
HANDS-ON TIME: 27 MIN.; TOTAL TIME: 1 HR., 57 MIN.

- 1 cup unsalted butter, softened
- 1½ cups powdered sugar, divided
- 2 Tbsp. frozen limeade concentrate, thawed
- ⅔ cup finely chopped pistachios
- 2 tsp. lime zest, divided
- ½ tsp. vanilla extract
- 2 cups all-purpose flour
- ⅛ tsp. salt

1. Beat butter, ½ cup powdered sugar, and limeade concentrate at medium speed with an electric mixer until creamy. Stir in nuts, 1 tsp. lime zest, and vanilla.
2. Whisk together flour and salt; gradually add to butter mixture, beating at medium speed until a soft dough forms. Cover and chill 1 hour.
3. Preheat oven to 375°. Shape dough into 1-inch balls, and place on ungreased baking sheets. Bake at 375° for 14 to 15 minutes or until lightly browned. Remove cookies to wire racks, and cool 5 minutes.
4. Stir together remaining 1 tsp. lime zest and remaining 1 cup powdered sugar; roll warm cookies in powdered sugar mixture, and cool completely on wire racks.

great gift

Candy Bar Sugar Cookies

MAKES 4 DOZEN
HANDS-ON TIME: 19 MIN.; TOTAL TIME: 1 HR., 13 MIN.

- ½ cup shortening
- ¼ cup butter, softened
- ½ cup firmly packed light brown sugar
- 1 large egg
- 1½ tsp. vanilla extract
- 2 cups all-purpose flour
- 1½ tsp. baking powder
- ½ tsp. baking soda
- ½ tsp. salt
- 2 (2.1-oz.) chocolate-covered crispy peanut-buttery candy bars, coarsely chopped (we tested with Butterfinger)
- 6 Tbsp. turbinado sugar
- Parchment paper

1. Preheat oven to 375°. Beat shortening and butter at medium speed with an electric mixer until creamy. Gradually add brown sugar, beating until smooth. Add egg and vanilla, beating until blended.

2. Combine flour and next 3 ingredients; gradually add to shortening mixture, beating just until blended. Stir in candy. Shape dough into 1-inch balls; roll each ball in turbinado sugar. Place balls 3 inches apart on parchment paper-lined baking sheets.

3. Bake at 375° for 9 to 10 minutes or until lightly browned. Cool 2 minutes on baking sheets; remove to wire racks to cool completely.

editor's favorite • great gift • make ahead

Orange Pralines

MAKES 2½ DOZEN
HANDS-ON TIME: 21 MIN.; TOTAL TIME: 21 MIN.

For a delightful gift of this New Orleans specialty, attach a copy of the recipe to a bottle of high-quality orange extract nestled in a basketful of these sweet treats.

- Wax paper
- 1¼ cups sugar
- 1 cup firmly packed dark brown sugar
- ½ cup heavy cream
- 6 Tbsp. unsalted butter
- ¾ cup chopped pecans, toasted
- ¾ cup pecan halves, toasted
- 1 tsp. orange extract (we tested with Massey)
- 2 tsp. orange zest

1. Lightly grease 1 (24-inch-long) sheet of wax paper; set aside.

2. Combine sugar and next 5 ingredients in a heavy 3-quart saucepan. Bring to a boil over medium heat, stirring constantly. Wash down crystals from sides of pan with a pastry brush dipped in hot water; insert a candy thermometer. Cook until thermometer registers 234° to 238° (soft ball stage), about 6 minutes, stirring occasionally.

3. Remove from heat, and stir in orange extract and zest. Beat with a wooden spoon 5 minutes or just until mixture begins to thicken and lose its gloss. Working rapidly, drop by table-spoonfuls onto prepared wax paper; let stand until firm.

spa GIFTS

Pamper everyone on your gift list with luxurious bath and body products that are simple to make. Many can be packaged in glass bottles and containers you recycle from your own pantry.

Scented Bath Salts

You can find essential oils at health food stores and bath shops. A wide variety is also available online.

MAKES 3 CUPS

2 cups Epsom salts
1 cup sea salt or rock salt
¼ tsp. glycerin
Essential oil, such as peppermint or citrus
Clear plastic acrylic fillable ball ornament or glass jar with tight-fitting lid

1. Combine salts in mixing bowl. Mix well.
2. Stir in glycerin and 4 to 5 drops of essential oil. Mix well.
3. Spoon bath salts into containers. Store any leftover bath salts in an airtight container.

To use, pour one-half cup of bath salts under running water when filling the bath.

Gardener's Hand Scrub

This scrub is perfect for a friend who likes to dig in the dirt.
MAKES 12 OZ.

Small pumice stone (approximately 5- x 1-inch)
1 cup grated bar soap
½ cup borax (available in detergent section of grocery
   stores)
Container with tight-fitting lid

1. Place pumice stone in a heavy-duty zip-top plastic bag, and seal. On a hard surface, use a hammer to smash the stone to a fine powder. You should have approximately ¼ cup of pumice powder.
2. Combine pumice powder, soap, and borax. Mix well. Pour into the container and replace the top.

To use, pour a small amount of hand scrub into hand, and mix with warm water to form a lather; rinse hands with warm water.

Lavender Eye Pillow

This fragrant eye pillow is a favorite gift during the hurried holidays.

- ¾   cup dried lavender
- ¾   cup dried buckwheat hulls
- 3   Tbsp. dried orris root chips per pillow
- 8   drops lavender essential oil per pillow
- ¼   yd. tightly woven natural fabric, such as silk

1. To make the lavender mix: Combine lavender and buckwheat hulls in a glass bowl. Make a well in the center of the mix, and add orris root. Pour essential oil onto the orris root chips, and stir the mixture. Place mixture in a sealed container in a cool, dark place for 2 weeks. After 2 weeks, the mixture is ready to fill eye pillows.

2. To make the eye pillow case: Cut two 8½- x 4-inch rectangles from fabric. (You may trim the rectangle into a heart shape, but be sure to keep the finished dimension 8- x 3½-inches.) With right sides facing, stitch around the rectangle ⅜-inch from the raw edge, leaving a 2-inch opening. Trim the seam, and turn the pillow right side out. Fill the pillow with the lavender mixture. Slipstitch the opening closed.

To use, give the pillow a squeeze, and place on eyes. Relax and enjoy!

Lavender-Rose Powder

Recycled glass spice bottles with removable perforated tops make ideal shakers for this fragrant powder.

MAKES 2 CUPS

- 1 cup talc
- 1 cup cornstarch
- 1/8 tsp. lavender essential oil
- 1/8 tsp. cinnamon essential oil
- 10 drops rose essential oil
- Wax paper
- Container, such as a clean, dry recycled glass spice jar with perforated top

1. Blend ingredients together. Let mixture dry on wax paper.
2. Spoon mixture into the container, and replace the top.

Vanilla Foaming Bath Oil

Avocado, almond, safflower, sunflower, or olive oil can be used to make bath oil, but mineral oil has the longest shelf life.

MAKES 16 OZ.

- 1 cup light vegetable oil
- 1/2 cup glycerin
- 1/2 cup mild liquid soap
- 1 Tbsp. vanilla extract
- Bottle with a tight-fitting lid

1. Stir together all ingredients until well blended. Pour into the bottle, and replace the top.
2. To use, shake well to reblend the ingredients. Pour 1/4 cup under running water when filling the bath.

Lavender Bath Oil

To allow the bath oils to blend, store for two weeks in a cool, dark place before giving as a gift.

MAKES 16 TO 24 OZ., DEPENDING ON SIZE OF BOTTLE

- Bottle with tight-fitting lid
- Sprigs of dried lavender and/or rosemary
- Enough mineral oil to fill bottle
- Lavender essential oil

1. Place desired number of herb sprigs in the bottle.
2. Using a funnel, fill the bottle with mineral oil. Add 4 to 5 drops of essential oil for a medium-size (about 16- to 24-oz.) bottle, and replace the top.
3. To use, shake well to reblend the ingredients. Pour 1/4 cup under running water when filling the bath.

Outdoorsman Aftershave

This aftershave has a pleasing, woodsy scent.

MAKES 8 OZ.

- 1 cup witch hazel
- 1/2 Tbsp. dried rosemary
- 1 tsp. vanilla extract
- 1 Tbsp. dried pine needles
- Bottle with a tight-fitting lid

1. Mix all ingredients until well blended. Pour into the container, and replace the top. Place the container in a cool, dark place for 2 weeks.
2. After 2 weeks, pour the liquid through a paper coffee filter-lined strainer to remove all solid ingredients. Pour the liquid into a bottle with a tight-fitting lid, and replace the lid.
3. To use, splash on face after shaving.

To label your spa gifts, write the product name on a small piece of handmade paper. Make a tiny hole in one end of the tag, and use raffia or ribbon to tie the tag to the bottle.

Love it? GET IT!

Many items pictured in the book are one-of-a-kind or no longer available—we've listed similar looks when possible. Source information is current at the time of publication. If an item is not listed, its source is unknown.

• page 11—**napkins, wooden charger:** Table Matters, Birmingham, AL, (205) 879-0125, www.table-matters.com

• page 13—**serving stand:** Pottery Barn, (888) 779-5176, www.potterybarn.com

• page 16—**square platter:** Pottery Barn, (888) 779-5176, www.potterybarn.com

• page 19—**individual trifle dishes:** Bed Bath & Beyond, (800) 462-3966, www.bedbathandbeyond.com

• page 21—**place mat:** Table Matters, Birmingham, AL, (205) 879-0125, www.table-matters.com

• page 27—**mugs:** Fortunata, www.fortunatainc.com

• page 29—**cactus containers:** Pottery Barn, (888) 779-5176, www.potterybarn.com; **candles, candle holders:** Lamb's Ears, Ltd., Birmingham, AL, (205) 969-3138, www.lambsearsltd.com

• page 32—**chip and dip dish:** A'Mano, Birmingham, AL, (205) 871-9093, www.amanogifts.com

• pages 36-37—**plate, bowls:** R. Wood Studio Ceramics, (888) 817-9663, www.rwoodstudio.com

• page 38—**plate:** A'Mano, Birmingham, AL, (205) 871-9093, www.amanogifts.com

• page 40—**napkin ring:** Pottery Barn, (888) 779-5176, www.potterybarn.com; **place mat:** Dransfield & Ross, www.dransfieldandross.biz

• page 51—**napkin:** Dransfield & Ross, www.dransfieldandross.biz

• page 53—**linens, place mats, glasses:** Table Matters, Birmingham, AL, (205) 879-0125, www.table-matters.com; **plate, charger:** Lamb's Ears, Ltd., Birmingham, AL, (205) 969-3138,

www.lambsearsltd.com; **wine glasses:** Bromberg & Co., Inc., Birmingham, AL, (205) 871-3276, www.brombergs.com; **votive holders and ornament:** Anthropologie, (800) 309-2500, www.anthropologie.com

• page 55—**salad plate:** Lamb's Ears, Ltd., Birmingham, AL, (205) 969-3138, www.lambsearsltd.com

• pages 56-57—**platter:** Table Matters, Birmingham, AL, (205) 879-0125, www.table-matters.com

• page 64—**tray:** Pottery Barn, (888) 779-5176, www.potterybarn.com

• page 67—**mugs:** Mariposa, (800) 788-1304, www.mariposa-gift.com

• page 69—**tiered server:** Pottery Barn, (888) 779-5176, www.potterybarn.com

• page 73—**pedestal:** Pottery Barn, (888) 779-5176, www.potterybarn.com

• page 79—**eggs, nest, owl:** Leaf & Petal, Birmingham, AL, (205) 877-3030, www.leafnpetal.com; **evergreen wreath:** Flowerbuds, Inc., Birmingham, AL, (205) 970-3223, www.flowerbudsinc.com; **ribbon:** Davis Wholesale Florist, www.daviswholesaleflorist.com

• page 80—**Eucalyptus wreath (undecorated):** Davis Wholesale Florist; www.daviswholesaleflorist.com

• pages 82-83: **vintage flatware with Christmas words:** Monkeys Always Look, www.monkeysalwayslookshop.com

• page 84—**ribbons:** Smith's Variety, Birmingham, AL, (205) 871-0841, www.smithsvarietyshop.com; **interior (black, white, and pink bedroom):** Dana Wolter Interiors, Birmingham, AL, (205) 563-5779, www.danawolterinteriors.com

• page 88—**silver chalk trays:** Frabbits/ Forrest Lights, (770) 992-2516, **stockings:** Garnet Hill, (800) 870-3513, www.garnethill.com; **fire screen:** At Home, Birmingham, AL, (205) 879-3510, www.athome-furnishings.com

• pages 92-93—**urns:** Leaf & Petal, Birmingham, AL, (205) 877-3030, www.leafnpetal.com; **mini urns:** Park Lane Flowers, Birmingham, AL, (205) 879-7115

• pages 98-99—**interiors (table settings):** Dana Wolter Interiors, Birmingham, AL, (205) 563-5779, www.danawolterinteriors.com

• pages 100-101—**ribbons:** Smith's Variety, Birmingham, AL, (205) 871-0841, www.smithsvarietyshop.com; **glass vases:** Flowerbuds, Inc., Birmingham, AL, (205) 970-3223, www.flowerbudsinc.com

• page 102—**candles:** At Home, Birmingham, AL, (205) 879-3510, www.athome-furnishings.com; **place mats:** Dransfield & Ross, www.dransfieldandross.biz

• page 103—**white tree:** A'Mano, Birmingham, AL, (205) 871-9093, www.amanogifts.com; **framed hand towel:** Art Goodies, www.artgoodiesonline.com

• pages 108-109—**interiors (branch tree with flowers, branch tree with paper chain):** Dana Wolter Interiors, Birmingham, AL, (205) 563-5779, www.danawolterinteriors.com

• page 112—**interior (lily floral arrangement):** Christopher Glenn, Inc., Birmingham, AL, (205) 870-1236, and Dana Wolter Interiors, Birmingham, AL, (205) 563-5779, www.danawolterinteriors.com; **interior** (silver vase floral arrangements): Caroline House/Briarwood Presbyterian Church, Birmingham, AL, (205) 776-5200

• page 114—**boxwood wreaths:** Flowerbuds, Inc., Birmingham, AL, (205) 970-3223, www.flowerbudsinc.com; **12 Days of Christmas ornaments:** Ballard, (800) 536-7551, www.ballarddesigns.com

• page 115—**red mercury glass trees:** At Home, Birmingham, AL, (205) 879-3510, www.athome-furnishings.com

• page 116—**stockings:** Horchow, www.horchow.com

• page 118—**basket, moss and lichen balls:** Leaf & Petal, Birmingham, AL, (205) 877-3030, www.leafnpetal.com

• page 119—**bowl:** Lamb's Ears, Ltd., Birmingham, AL, (205) 969-3138, www.lambsearsltd.com; **pine cone lights:** Flowerbuds, Inc., Birmingham, AL,

(205) 970-3223, www.flowerbudsinc.com

• page 122—**snowflake forks:** Target, (800) 591-3869, www.target.com

• page 124—**star plates:** Pottery Barn, (888) 779-5176, www.potterybarn.com

• page 126—**plate:** Vietri, (919) 245-4180, www.vietri.com; **red casserole dish:** Revol, (888) 337-3865, www.revol-usa.com

• page 129—**place mat:** Vietri, (919) 245-4180, www.vietri.com; **plate:** A'Mano, Birmingham, AL, (205) 871-9093, www.amanogifts.com

• page 134—**linen:** Table Matters, Birmingham, AL, (205) 879-0125, www.table-matters.com

• page 137—**plate:** Anthropologie, (800) 309-2500, www.anthropologie.com; **tartlet tray:** Lamb's Ears, Ltd., Birmingham, AL, (205) 969-3138,

www.lambsearsltd.com

• page 140—**linen:** Table Matters, Birmingham, AL, (205) 879-0125, www.table-matters.com

• page 141—**glass dessert dishes:** Vietri, (919) 245-4180, www.vietri.com; **linen:** Table Matters, Birmingham, AL, (205) 879-0125, www.table-matters.com

• page 144—**casserole dish:** Vietri, (919) 245-4180, www.vietri.com

• page 145—**mugs:** World Market, (877) 967-5362, www.worldmarket.com

• page 148—**flatware:** Pottery Barn, (888) 779-5176, www.potterybarn.com

• page 157—**containers:** A'Mano, Birmingham, AL, (205) 871-9093, www.amanogifts.com

• page 159—**box:** Michaels, (800) 642-4235, www.michaels.com

* *

Thanks to these CONTRIBUTORS

Editorial contributors

Margaret Agnew
Ana Price Kelly
Laurl Self
Dana Wolter
Caroline Markunas Wright

Thanks to the following homeowners

Judy & Craig Beatty
Katherine & John Cobbs
Katherine & David Coyne
Cheryl & William Miller
Ashley & Ken Polk
Melanie & Michael Pounds
Dana & Daniel Wolter

Thanks to these Birmingham businesses

A'Mano
At Home Furnishings
Bromberg & Co., Inc.
Christine's
Davis Wholesale Flowers
Flowerbuds, Inc.
Henhouse Antiques
Lamb's Ears, Ltd.
Leaf & Petal
Mulberry Heights Antiques
Park Lane Flowers
Pottery Barn
Smith's Variety Shop
Table Matters
Tricia's Treasures

GENERAL INDEX

METRIC EQUIVALENTS

The recipes that appear in this cookbook use the standard U.S. method for measuring liquid and dry or solid ingredients (teaspoons, tablespoons, and cups). The information in the following charts is provided to help cooks outside the United States successfully use these recipes. All equivalents are approximate.

Metric Equivalents for Different Types of Ingredients

A standard cup measure of a dry or solid ingredient will vary in weight depending on the type of ingredient. A standard cup of liquid is the same volume for any type of liquid. Use the following chart when converting standard cup measures to grams (weight) or milliliters (volume).

Standard Cup	Fine Powder (ex. flour)	Grain (ex. rice)	Granular (ex. sugar)	Liquid Solids (ex. butter)	Liquid (ex. milk)
1	140 g	150 g	190 g	200 g	240 ml
¾	105 g	113 g	143 g	150 g	180 ml
⅔	93 g	100 g	125 g	133 g	160 ml
½	70 g	75 g	95 g	100 g	120 ml
⅓	47 g	50 g	63 g	67 g	80 ml
¼	35 g	38 g	48 g	50 g	60 ml
⅛	18 g	19 g	24 g	25 g	30 ml

Useful Equivalents for Dry Ingredients by Weight
(To convert ounces to grams, multiply the number of ounces by 30.)

1 oz	=	1/16 lb	=	30 g
4 oz	=	¼ lb	=	120 g
8 oz	=	½ lb	=	240 g
12 oz	=	¾ lb	=	360 g
16 oz	=	1 lb	=	480 g

Useful Equivalents for Length
(To convert inches to centimeters, multiply the number of inches by 2.5.)

1 in				=	2.5 cm		
6 in	=	½ ft		=	15 cm		
12 in	=	1 ft		=	30 cm		
36 in	=	3 ft	=	1 yd	=	90 cm		
40 in				=	100 cm	=	1 m

Useful Equivalents for Liquid Ingredients by Volume

¼ tsp					=	1 ml
½ tsp					=	2 ml
1 tsp					=	5 ml
3 tsp	=	1 Tbsp		=	½ fl oz	=	15 ml
		2 Tbsp	=	⅛ cup	=	1 fl oz	=	30 ml
		4 Tbsp	=	¼ cup	=	2 fl oz	=	60 ml
		5⅓ Tbsp	=	⅓ cup	=	3 fl oz	=	80 ml
		8 Tbsp	=	½ cup	=	4 fl oz	=	120 ml
		10⅔ Tbsp	=	⅔ cup	=	5 fl oz	=	160 ml
		12 Tbsp	=	¾ cup	=	6 fl oz	=	180 ml
		16 Tbsp	=	1 cup	=	8 fl oz	=	240 ml
		1 pt	=	2 cups	=	16 fl oz	=	480 ml
		1 qt	=	4 cups	=	32 fl oz	=	960 ml
						33 fl oz	=	1000 ml = 1 l

Useful Equivalents for Cooking/Oven Temperatures

	Fahrenheit	Celsius	Gas Mark
Freeze water	32° F	0° C	
Room temperature	68° F	20° C	
Boil water	212° F	100° C	
Bake	325° F	160° C	3
	350° F	180° C	4
	375° F	190° C	5
	400° F	200° C	6
	425° F	220° C	7
	450° F	230° C	8
Broil			Grill

RECIPE INDEX

HOLIDAY PLANNER

Getting ready for the holiday season is half of the fun!
From decorating the house to entertaining guests, this helpful
planner makes organizing easy. It's also a good reference when you
start making plans for next year's Christmas.

NOVEMBER *2010*

Sunday	Monday	Tuesday	Wednesday
	1	2	3
7	8	9	10
14	15	16	17
21	22	23	24
28	29	30	

Thursday	Friday	Saturday
4	5	6
11	12	13
18	19	20
Thanksgiving 25	26	27

Holiday-Ready Pantry

Be prepared for seasonal cooking and baking by stocking up on these items.

☐ Assorted coffees, teas, hot chocolate, and eggnog
☐ Wine, beer, and soft drinks
☐ White, brown, and powdered sugars
☐ Ground allspice, cinnamon, cloves, ginger, and nutmeg
☐ Baking soda and baking powder
☐ Seasonal fresh herbs
☐ Baking chocolate
☐ Semisweet chocolate morsels
☐ Assorted nuts
☐ Flaked coconut
☐ Sweetened condensed milk and evaporated milk
☐ Whipping cream
☐ Jams, jellies, and preserves
☐ Raisins, cranberries, and other fresh or dried fruits
☐ Canned pumpkin
☐ Frozen/refrigerated bread dough, biscuits, and croissants

Holiday Hotlines

Use these toll-free telephone numbers when you need answers to last-minute food questions.

- USDA Meat & Poultry Hotline: 1-800-535-4555
- FDA Center for Food Safety: 1-888-723-3366
- Butterball Turkey Talk Line: 1-800-288-8372
- The Reynolds Turkey Tips Hotline: 1-800-745-4500
- Betty Crocker (General Mills): 1-888-275-2388

DECEMBER *2010*

Sunday	Monday	Tuesday	Wednesday
			1
5	6	7	8
12	13	14	15
19	20	21	22
26	27	28	29

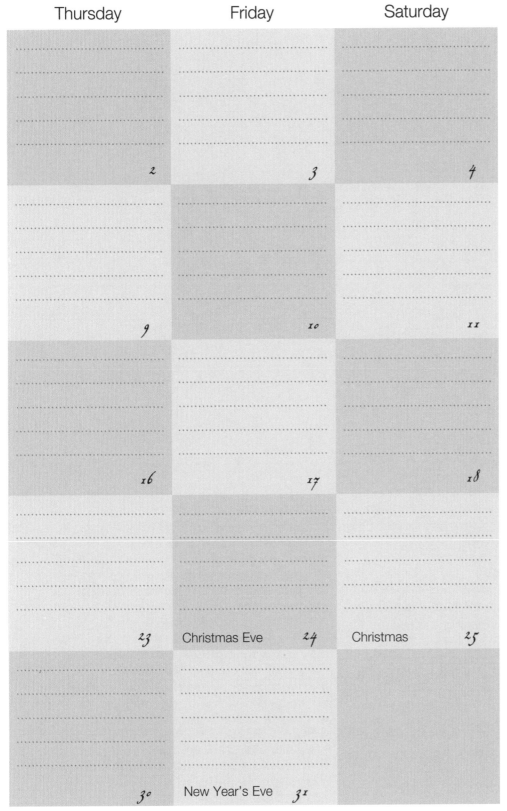

Thursday	Friday	Saturday
2	3	4
9	10	11
16	17	18
23	Christmas Eve 24	Christmas 25
30	New Year's Eve 31	

Helpful Hostess Tips

Use these shortcuts and tips to make your holiday get-togethers go off without a hitch.

- Always expect the unexpected. Should red wine spill, be prepared with your favorite stain remover. We love Wine Away, available through www.drugstore.com.
- In case it rains, keep a few extra umbrellas on hand so your friends don't get soaked running to their cars.
- Think about parking ahead of time. Too many extra cars on the street can be dangerous. Check with your neighbors to see if their driveways may be available.
- If someone asks to help, don't be afraid to take them up on the generous offer.
- Ask friends to arrive with a few of their favorite CDs so you have an eclectic collection to choose from.
- A little prep work goes a long way. Before guests arrive, uncork all the wine bottles, light candles, and put coffee and water in your machine.
- Double-check that you have plenty of extra hangers in your coat closet. Or use a spare bedroom to store coats, hats, and purses.
- When hosting a large crowd, consider renting china, silverware, glasses, and more from a local party or event store. You'll be amazed at how low the prices are if you stick to the basics.

Decorating PLANNER

Use this planner to decide what you'll need to spread holiday cheer through your house this year.

Decorative materials needed

from the yard ....

....

from around the house ....

....

from the store ....

....

other ....

Holiday decorations

for the table ....

....

for the door ....

....

for the mantel ....

....

for the staircase ....

....

other ....

Your Best Christmas Tree Ever

Several tricks can make your tree sparkle better than ever. Invite these ideas into your tree-trimming traditions, and then sit back and enjoy your gorgeous work of art.

• Skip the Usual Metal Stand

This year, use a natural woven basket to hold your Christmas tree. You'll likely still need to support the trunk inside the basket with a stand, but the results are much more beautiful.

• More Bang with Bulbs

Lighting the tree doesn't have to be the dreaded task of the season. Go ahead and spring for new lights—there's a much better chance they'll work. Mix large bulbs with smaller ones for extra twinkle, and be sure to use a surge protector with multiple outlets so you don't overload your receptacles with a gaggle of extension cords. Place the lights on your tree at night so it's easier to see where you need to add or take away a strand. Another tip: When you decide where you want your tree to stand, wind twinkle lights—top to bottom—in the middle of the room; then scoot it into a corner or up against a window.

• The Real Fun Begins

Start with your largest ornaments first and arrange them all around the tree. If they're extra heavy, secure them to the tree with florist wire. Sometimes oversize baubles tend to slip off branches. Tie inexpensive Christmas balls and metallic jingle bells together with florist wire to create a bold cluster of color.

• Update Your Look

Give your tree a fresh look year after year by editing your ornaments. Maybe you want a color theme, such as all red and gold; then display the rest around the house.

• Experiment with Christmas Tree Toppers

Bunch fresh holly from the yard and large gold temple bells on top of the tree for a bold use of traditional materials. Fresh flowers are another nice decorating alternative to the traditional star. Or try a bold oversize bow in red velvet.

• Final Touches for a Fantastic Tree

When you're just about done, add some festive ribbon! Use as many colors as you like. Weave ribbon streamers down and around your tree, and secure with florist wire in a few spots.

Deck the HALLS!

Bring joy and merriment into your home with these fun and easy decorating ideas.

• Add Color to Your Front Door
Accent a bright white door with the deep colors of an evergreen wreath and garland. Tie on extra-wide red ribbons to complete the Christmas look and add graphic punch. Twinkling lights add a soft glow at night and allow the door and decor to be seen from the street.

• Picture-Perfect Garland
Deck your halls with a distinctive—and decidedly charming—family photo garland. Just cut circular shapes from copies of your favorite photos, and glue them to the backs of wooden curtain rings. Use ribbon to attach the rings to a garland for your stairs or mantel. You could even hang them on your tree. No doubt, Santa will feel most welcome when he sees all those smiling faces.

• Fill Cylinders with Ornaments
Use spray paint to add a shimmery touch to pinecones, acorns, or round glass ornaments. Displayed en masse in tall glass vases, they become instant and easy Christmas accents.

• Put Out Pretty Pillows
Make a quick switch from everyday to holiday by swapping out your throw pillows. It's an easy and affordable way to redecorate a room and change your look for the Christmas season.

• String Lights and Greenery
Disguise unsightly wires from string lights by winding them around a column or post with Christmas greenery or garland.

• Create an Arrangement with Fruit and Greenery
Use a glass hurricane or vase to create an arrangement that will last throughout the Christmas season by filling the jar with a layer of limes, red holly berries, and orange citrus. Top it off with stems of greenery.

• White and Bright
Here's a Christmas surprise: lilies for your dining room table. Though usually associated with spring, these crisp, snowy flowers with their star-shaped blooms couldn't be more perfect for yuletide celebrations. Available year-round, they add elegance and fragrance to any setting. To create an arrangement, buy one long stem from a local florist. Look for a stem that has one bloom open and several others beginning to unfurl. Clip the flowers from the stem, and place them in a vase. Add water daily, and the flowers should last for a week.

• Festive Floor Pillows
Create a comfy spot for kids to open presents on Christmas morning! Whip out your sewing machine and make a set of festive floor cushions, monogrammed with children's names.

Gift giving has never been so easy! Try these creative tips when it's time to start wrapping.

• Get Organized
Handy over-the-door closet organizers are good for more than just keeping track of shoes. Get one with clear plastic pockets, and fill it with present-wrapping necessities. (The best part: no more disappearing scissors and rolls of tape!) Stock gift tags, ribbon, bows, box toppers, tissue paper, and even small gifts, such as candles, that you can grab at the last minute. Whenever you're running low, restock items so you're never out of something when you need it most.

• That Special Gift
With a few more minutes and a little bit of creative fun, you can make your gifts unique and individual. Instead of buying another roll of wrapping paper, make your own. Use stamps and paint to transform recycled craft paper. It'll save you money, help the environment, and add memorable personality to every gift you give during the holiday season.

• Adorn Your Gifts
Pretty up your presents by attaching bells or ornaments. Use the same color ribbon on all your packages under the tree to make a cohesive look with different patterned wrapping papers.

• Make It Personal
You've found the perfect wine to bring as a hostess gift to your next holiday party, so don't just slip the bottle into a premade bag. Instead, make your gift more memorable. All you need are four or five strands of beaded wire, which you can purchase at a crafts store. Wrap the strands together to form a tiny wreath, and slide it over the neck of the bottle. Add a simple tag with a handwritten note to complete the festive look.

• Get Creative with Gift Tags
Don't bother buying more gift tags. Save money by making your own. Make color copies of tartan fabric, and cut it into rectangles to create festive gift tags. Or recycle last year's Christmas cards. Cut them into simple shapes, and use a grommet-maker or hole punch to add a small hole at one end or corner. Thread twine through the hole, and tie to the gift for a creative look.

• Say "Thanks for Coming" with Cookies
Print your favorite cookie recipe and baking instructions on white paper or vellum, and tie it around a frozen log of dough wrapped in parchment. When your guests are leaving, send them home with this easy Christmas gift they'll enjoy for days to come.

Party PLANNER

Holiday entertaining is a cinch when you use this planning chart to coordinate your party menu.

guests	what they're bringing	serving pieces needed
....	☐ appetizer ☐ beverage ☐ bread ☐ main dish ☐ side dish ☐ dessert	....
....	☐ appetizer ☐ beverage ☐ bread ☐ main dish ☐ side dish ☐ dessert	....
....	☐ appetizer ☐ beverage ☐ bread ☐ main dish ☐ side dish ☐ dessert	....
....	☐ appetizer ☐ beverage ☐ bread ☐ main dish ☐ side dish ☐ dessert	....
....	☐ appetizer ☐ beverage ☐ bread ☐ main dish ☐ side dish ☐ dessert	....
....	☐ appetizer ☐ beverage ☐ bread ☐ main dish ☐ side dish ☐ dessert	....
....	☐ appetizer ☐ beverage ☐ bread ☐ main dish ☐ side dish ☐ dessert	....
....	☐ appetizer ☐ beverage ☐ bread ☐ main dish ☐ side dish ☐ dessert	....
....	☐ appetizer ☐ beverage ☐ bread ☐ main dish ☐ side dish ☐ dessert	....
....	☐ appetizer ☐ beverage ☐ bread ☐ main dish ☐ side dish ☐ dessert	....
....	☐ appetizer ☐ beverage ☐ bread ☐ main dish ☐ side dish ☐ dessert	....
....	☐ appetizer ☐ beverage ☐ bread ☐ main dish ☐ side dish ☐ dessert	....
....	☐ appetizer ☐ beverage ☐ bread ☐ main dish ☐ side dish ☐ dessert	....
....	☐ appetizer ☐ beverage ☐ bread ☐ main dish ☐ side dish ☐ dessert	....
....	☐ appetizer ☐ beverage ☐ bread ☐ main dish ☐ side dish ☐ dessert	....

Party Guest List

....
....
....
....
....
....
....
....
....
....
....
....
....
....
....
....
....

Pantry List

Party To-Do List

....
....
....
....
....
....
....
....
....
....
....
....

Christmas Dinner PLANNER

Work on your menu, to-do list, and guest list for your holiday feast with this easy meal planner.

Menu Ideas

....
....
....
....
....
....
....

Dinner To-Do List

....
....
....
....
....
....
....

Christmas Dinner Guest List

....
....
....
....
....
....
....
....
....

Mix-and-Match MENUS

Menus below are based on recipes in the book.

CHRISTMAS EVE COCKTAIL AFFAIR

Sweet Tea and Limoncello Martinis (3x) (page 12)

Sparkling Cosmopolitan (2x) (page 66)

Minty Green Pea and Butter Bean Hummus (2x) (page 132)

Double Cheese Tartlets (page 136)

Quick Pot Stickers With Chinese Dipping Sauce (2x) (page 135)

Lamb Sliders With Mint-Garlic Mayonnaise (3x) (page 12)

White Chocolate-Key Lime Cheesecake Squares (2x) (page 68)

Orange Pralines (page 165)

Serves 30

CHRISTMAS MORNING BRUNCH BUFFET

Asiago, Mushroom, and Sausage Strata (page 125)

Christmas Morning Baked Cheese Grits (page 128)

Hot Curried Fruit Bake (page 131)

Brown Sugar-Cinnamon Coffee Cake With Spiced Streusel Topping (page 130)

Coffee, tea, and hot chocolate

Orange juice

Champagne

Serves 8

SPECIAL OCCASION DINNER

Mixed Citrus Compote (page 141)

Chicken Divan (page 146)

Mixed greens salad

Ambrosia Cake (page 143)

Serves 8

MEAT-AND-POTATOES SUPPER

Pan-Roasted Pork Tenderloin (page 57)

Crispy Sage and Garlic Smashed Baby Red Potatoes (page 17)

Mixed greens salad

Dinner rolls

Serves 8

LADIES ELEGANT LUNCHEON

Coconut-Lime Shrimp With Sweet Lime-Mustard Sauce (3x) (page 139)

Hearts of Romaine with Molasses Vinaigrette and Parmesan-Pancetta Crisps (page 14)

Roasted Meyer Lemon-Peppercorn Game Hens (page 15)

Citrus-Glazed Orange Rolls (page 140)

Pistachio-Lime Wedding Cookies (page 164)

Serves 12

DECADENT DESSERT PARTY

Pecan Caramel-Rum Tart (2x) (page 151)

Chocolate Chunk Cheesecake (2x) (page 20)

Petite Persimmon Puffs (page 68)

Candy Bar Sugar Cookies (page 165)

Hot Mocha (2x) (page 26)

Serves 20

Gifts AND Greetings

Record sizes and gifts in the chart below to make gift-shopping a breeze this holiday season. Write names and addresses on the facing page, and refer to it when it comes time to send Christmas cards.

Gift List and Size Charts

name /sizes	gift purchased/made	sent/delivered

name ....

jeans_____ shirt_____ sweater_____ jacket_____ shoes_____ belt_____

blouse_____ skirt_____ slacks_____ dress_____ suit_____ coat_____

pajamas_____ robe_____ hat_____ gloves_____ ring_____

name ....

jeans_____ shirt_____ sweater_____ jacket_____ shoes_____ belt_____

blouse_____ skirt_____ slacks_____ dress_____ suit_____ coat_____

pajamas_____ robe_____ hat_____ gloves_____ ring_____

name ....

jeans_____ shirt_____ sweater_____ jacket_____ shoes_____ belt_____

blouse_____ skirt_____ slacks_____ dress_____ suit_____ coat_____

pajamas_____ robe_____ hat_____ gloves_____ ring_____

name ....

jeans_____ shirt_____ sweater_____ jacket_____ shoes_____ belt_____

blouse_____ skirt_____ slacks_____ dress_____ suit_____ coat_____

pajamas_____ robe_____ hat_____ gloves_____ ring_____

name ....

jeans_____ shirt_____ sweater_____ jacket_____ shoes_____ belt_____

blouse_____ skirt_____ slacks_____ dress_____ suit_____ coat_____

pajamas_____ robe_____ hat_____ gloves_____ ring_____

name ....

jeans_____ shirt_____ sweater_____ jacket_____ shoes_____ belt_____

blouse_____ skirt_____ slacks_____ dress_____ suit_____ coat_____

pajamas_____ robe_____ hat_____ gloves_____ ring_____

name ....

jeans_____ shirt_____ sweater_____ jacket_____ shoes_____ belt_____

blouse_____ skirt_____ slacks_____ dress_____ suit_____ coat_____

pajamas_____ robe_____ hat_____ gloves_____ ring_____

Christmas Card List

name	address	sent/delivered

HOLIDAY *Memories*

Use these pages to reflect on your favorite holiday moments with family and friends.

Treasured Traditions

Keep track of your family's favorite holiday customs and pastimes on these lines.

....

....

....

....

....

....

....

....

....

....

....

....

....

....

Special Holiday Activities

What holiday events do you look forward to year after year? Write them down here.

....

....

....

....

....

....

....

....

Holiday Visits and Visitors

Keep a list of this year's holiday visitors. Jot down friend
and family news as well.

....
....
....
....
....
....
....
....
....
....
....
....
....
....
....
....
....
....
....
....
....
....
....
....
....
....

This Year's Favorite Recipes

Appetizers and Beverages ....
....
....
....
....
....

Entrées ....
....
....
....

Sides and Salads ....
....
....
....

Cookies and Candies ....
....
....
....

Desserts ....
....
....
....

Looking AHEAD

Holiday Wrap-up

Use this checklist to record thank you notes sent for holiday gifts and hospitality.

name	gift and/or event	note sent
....	....	☐
....	....	☐
....	....	☐
....	....	☐
....	....	☐
....	....	☐
....	....	☐
....	....	☐
....	....	☐
....	....	☐
....	....	☐
....	....	☐
....	....	☐

Notes for Next Year

Write down your ideas for Christmas 2011 on the lines below.

....

....

....

....

....

....

....

....

....